The Ultimate Ukulele Songbook

ISBN 978-1-4803-6032-7

HAL•LEONARD® CORPORATION

7777 W. BLUEMOUND RD. P.O. BOX 13819 MILWAUKEE, WI 53213

Visit Hal Leonard Online at
www.halleonard.com

The Ultimate Ukulele Songbook

NOTE-FOR-NOTE TRANSCRIPTIONS

STRUM & SING

UKULELE WITH TAB

SOLO UKULELE

UKULELE RIFFS

Hallelujah

Words and Music by Leonard Cohen

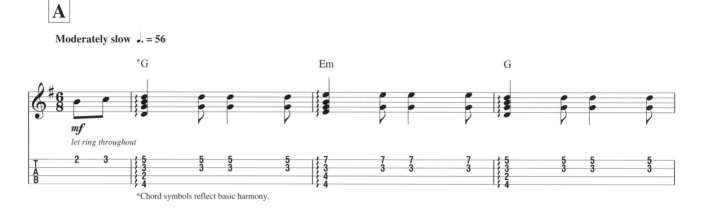

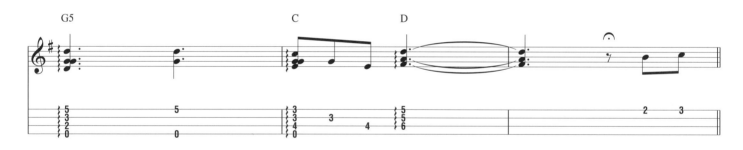

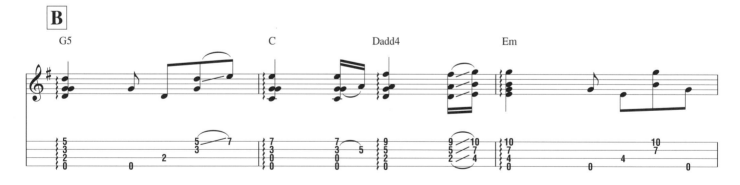

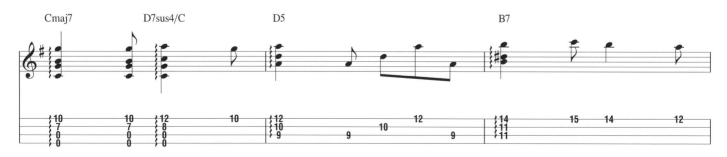

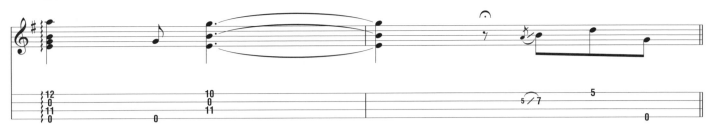

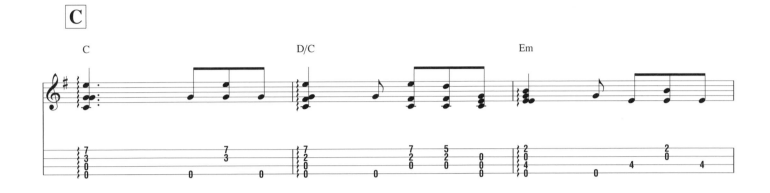

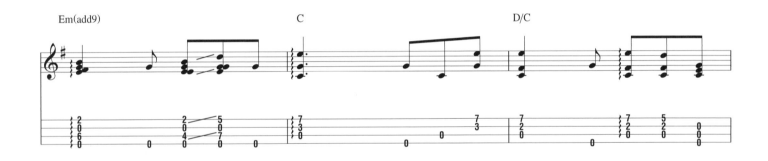

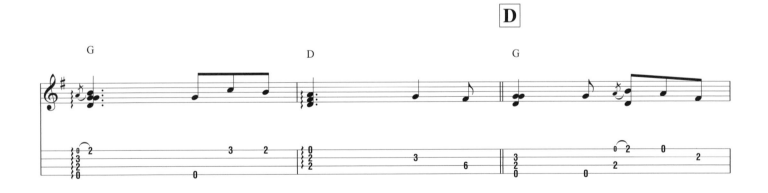

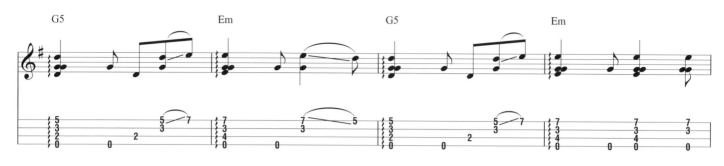

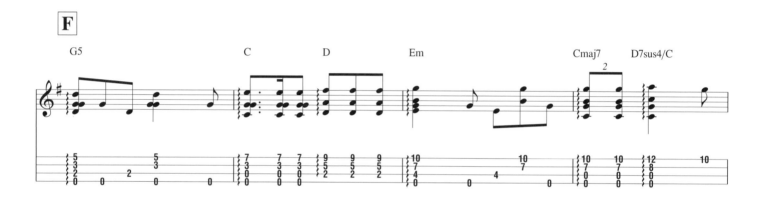

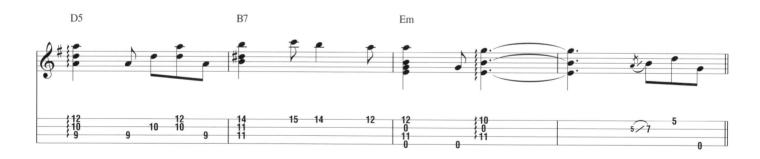

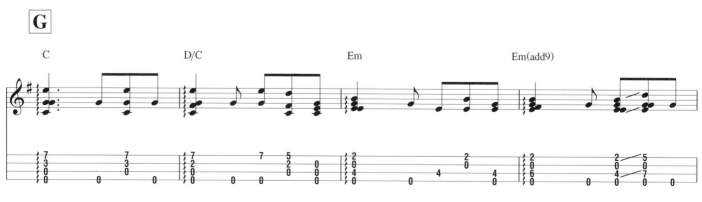

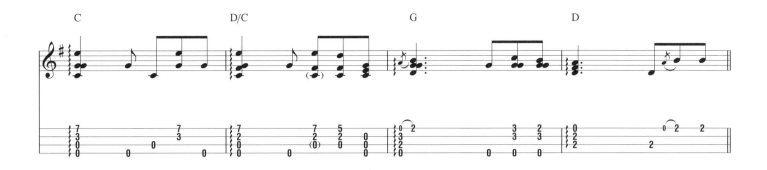

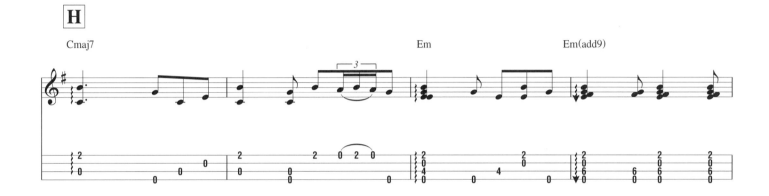

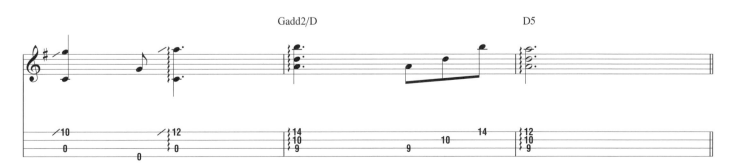

I

J

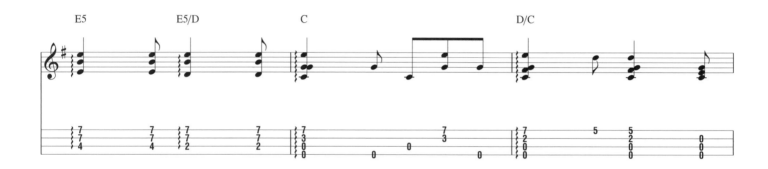

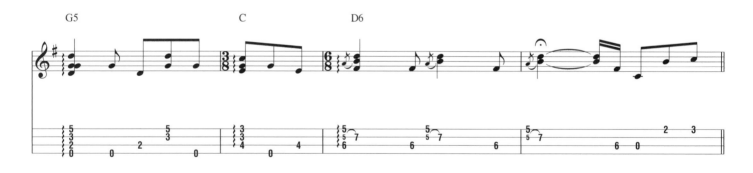

K

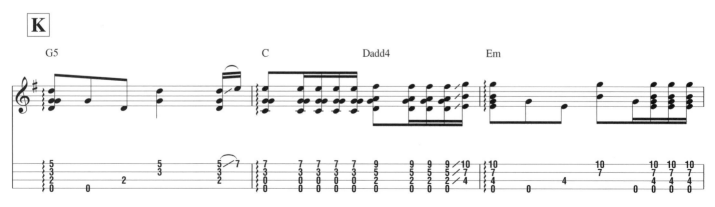

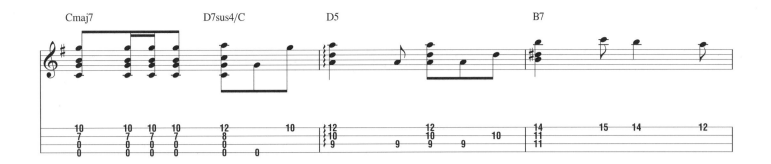

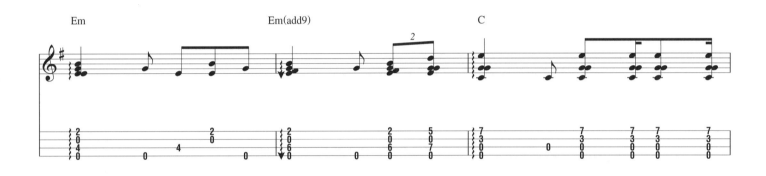

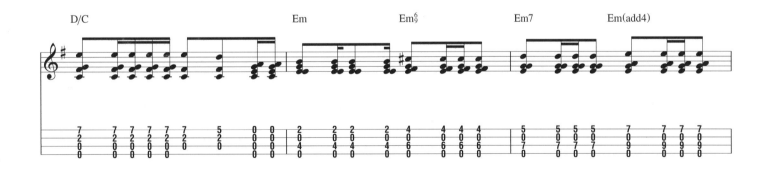

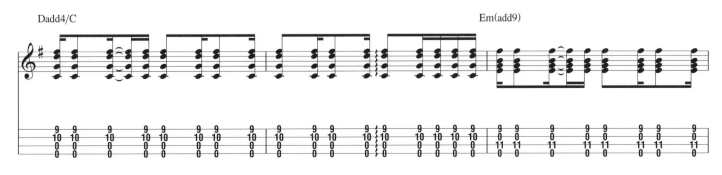

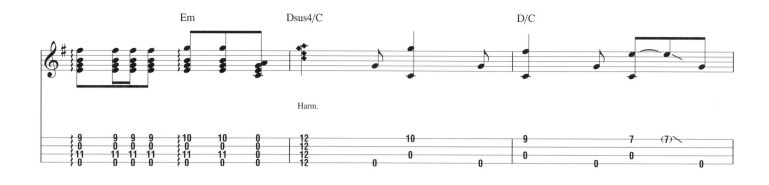

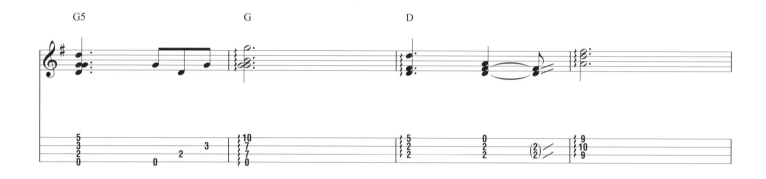

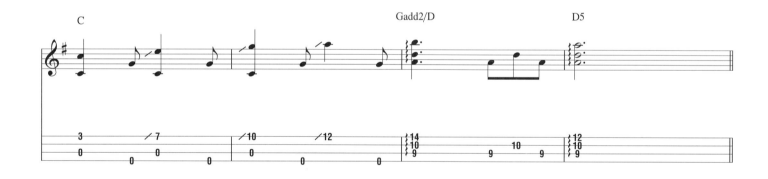

Spain

By Chick Corea

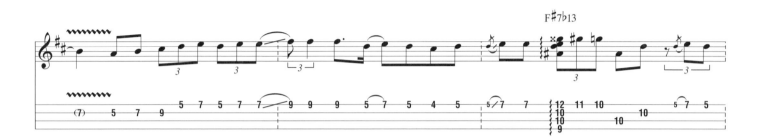

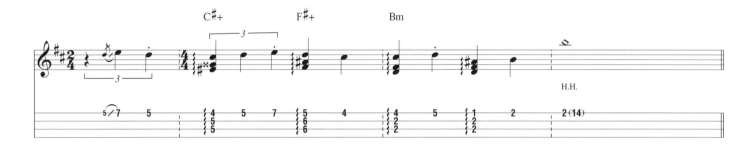

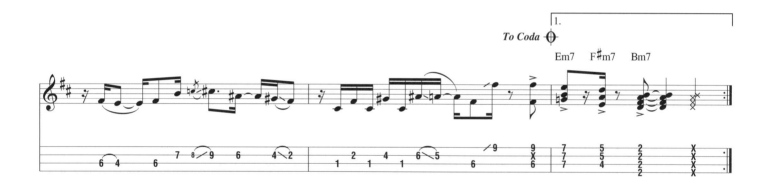

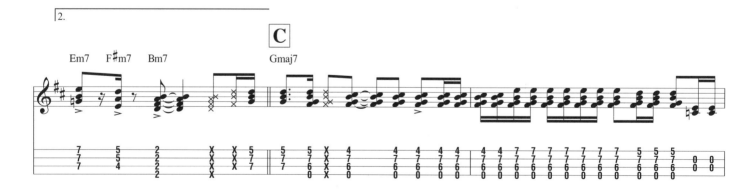

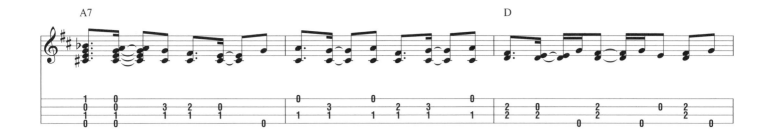

D

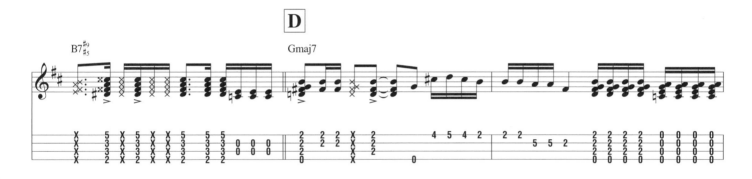

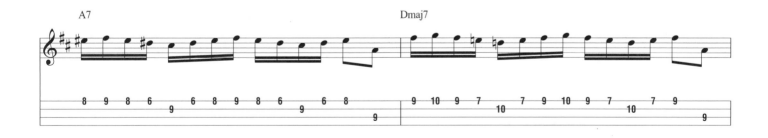

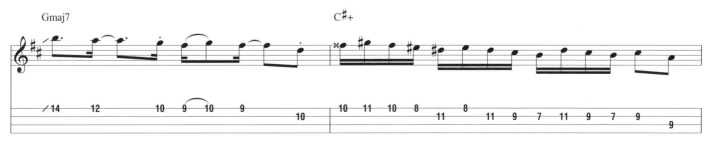

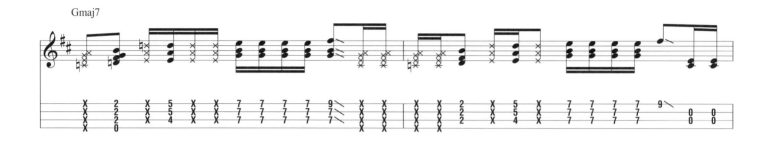

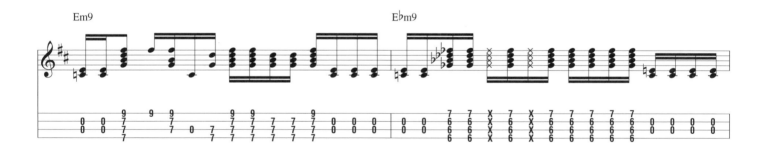

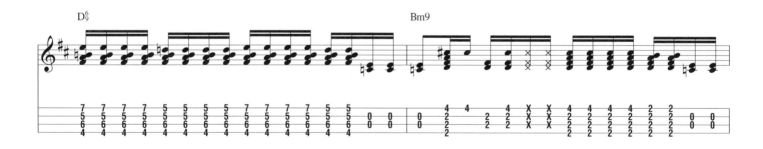

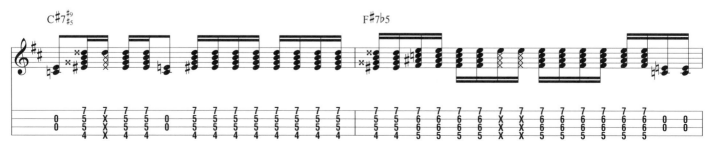

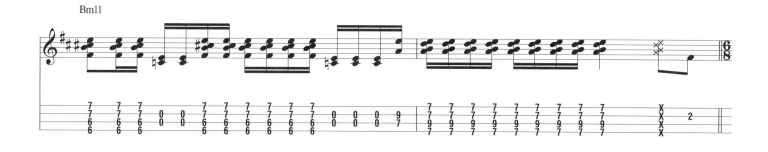

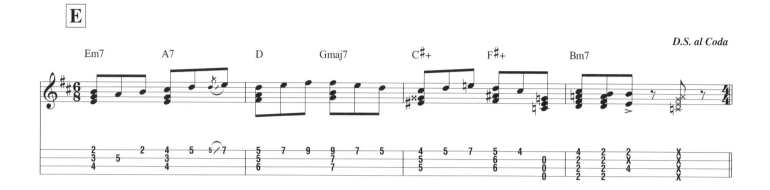

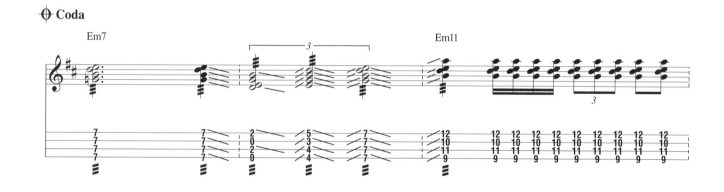

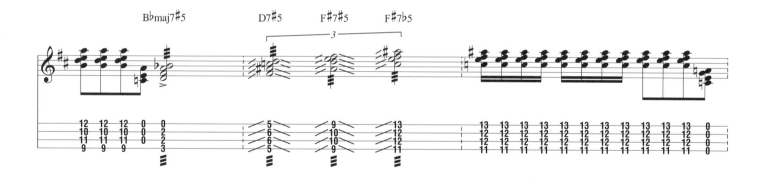

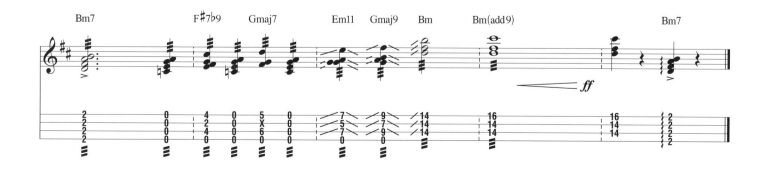

Kiss from a Rose

Words and Music by Seal

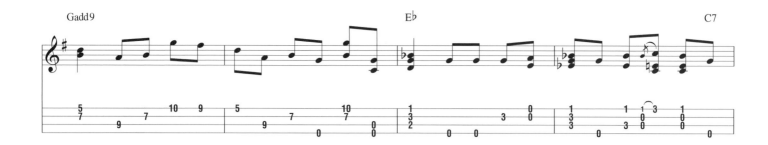

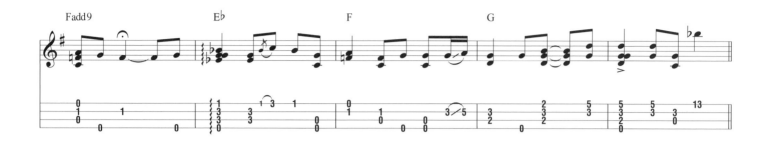

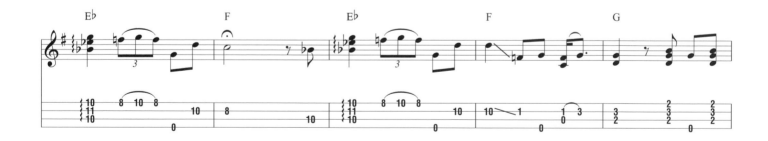

D

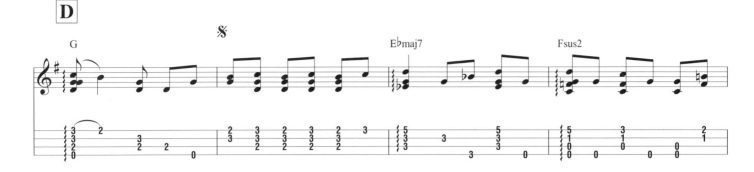

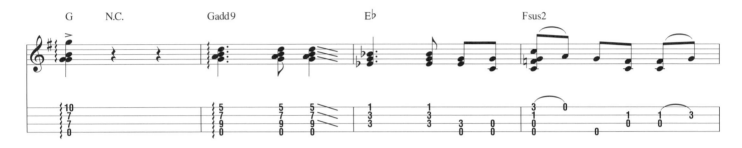

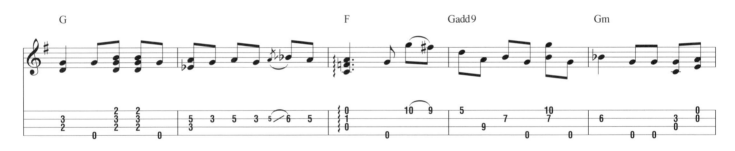

E

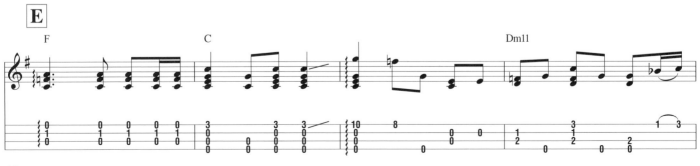

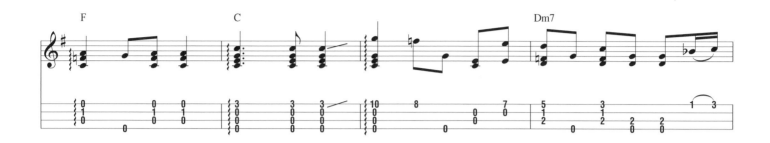

D.S. al Coda

⊕ Coda

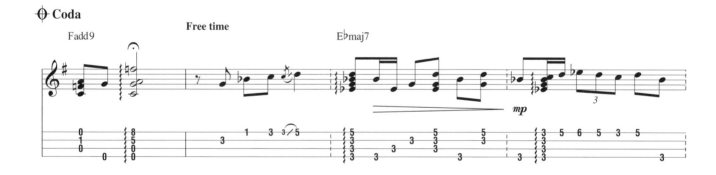

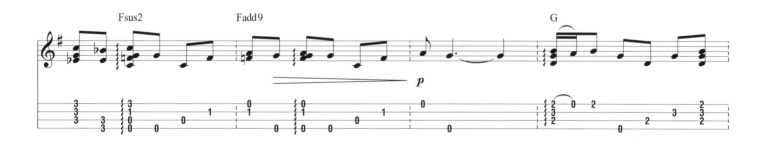

Tiger Rag
(Hold That Tiger)

Words by Harry DeCosta
Music by Original Dixieland Jazz Band

Tenor Banjo tuning (low to high): C-G-D-A

Fast ♩ = 170

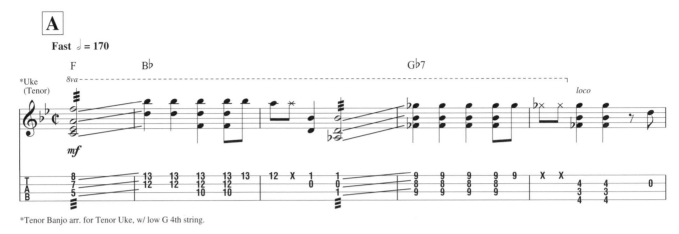

*Uke (Tenor)

*Tenor Banjo arr. for Tenor Uke, w/ low G 4th string.

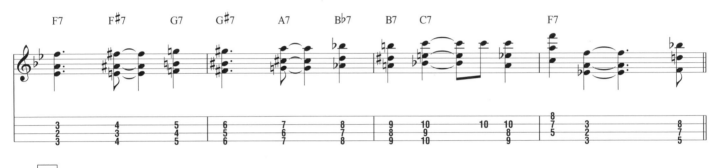

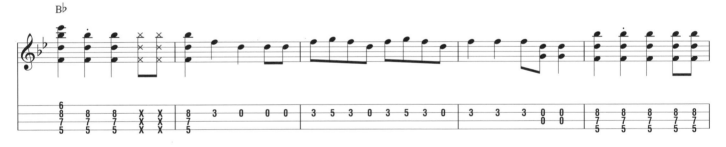

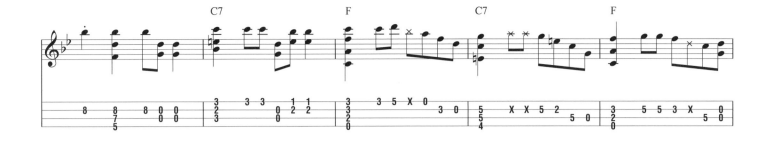

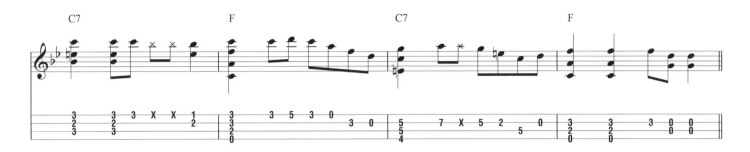

C

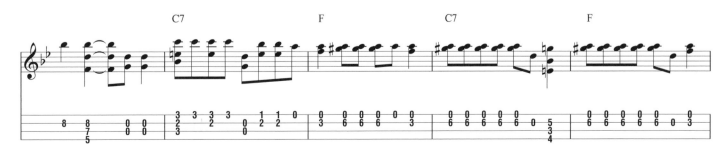

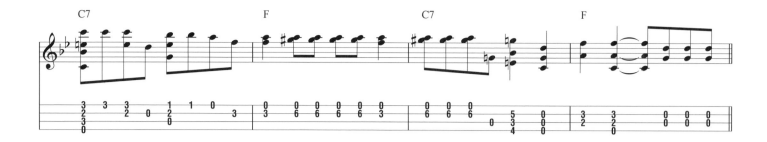

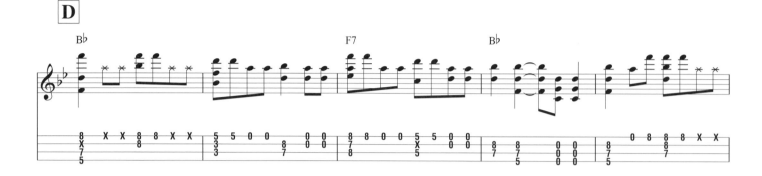

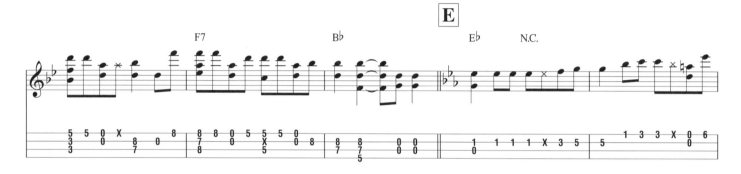

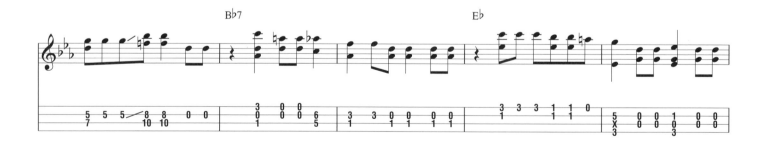

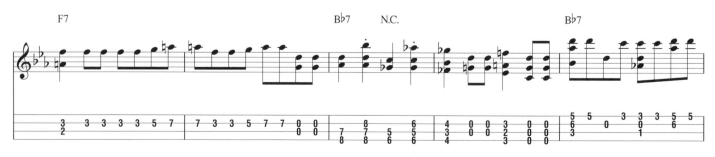

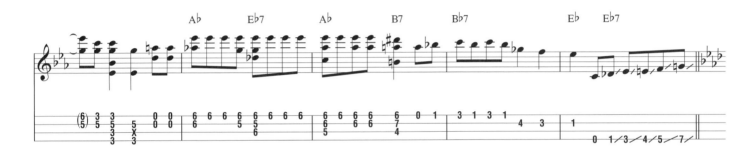

F

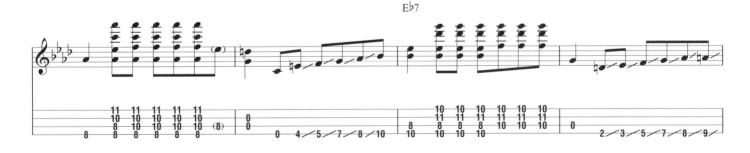

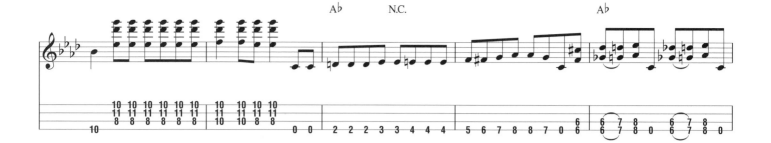

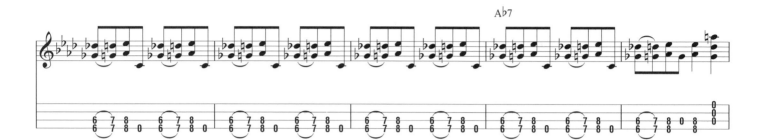

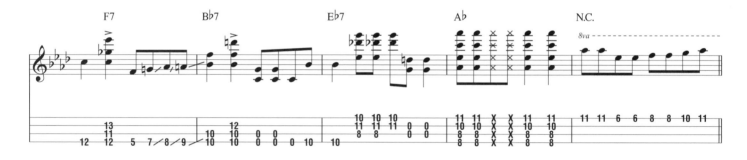

G

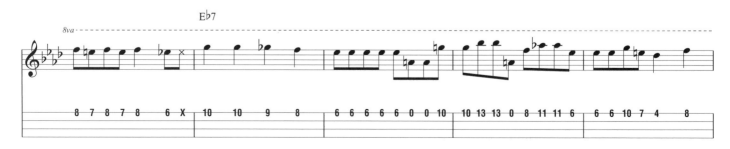

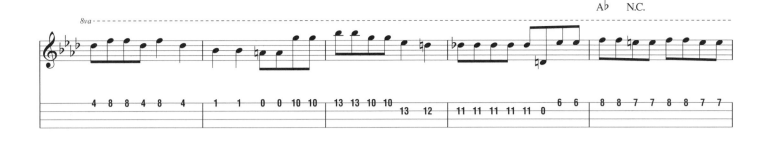

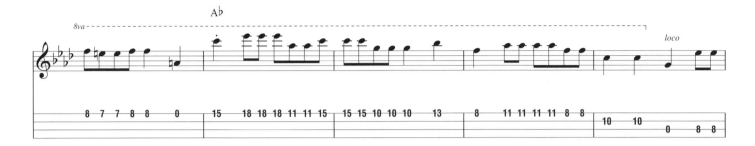

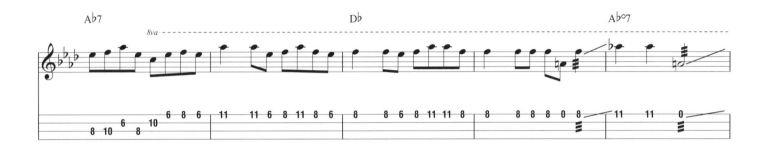

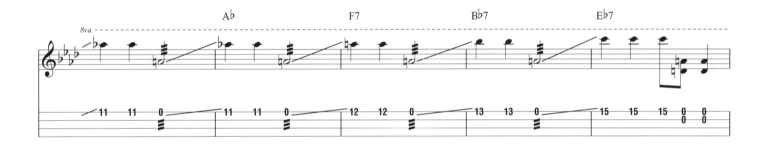

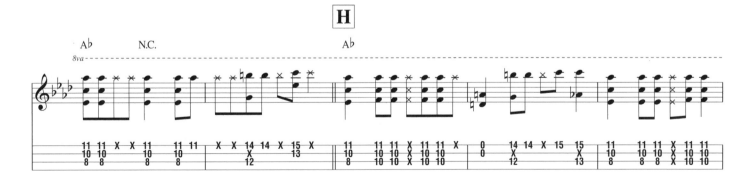

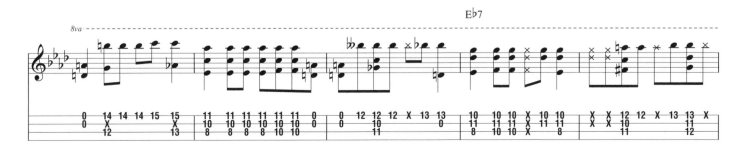

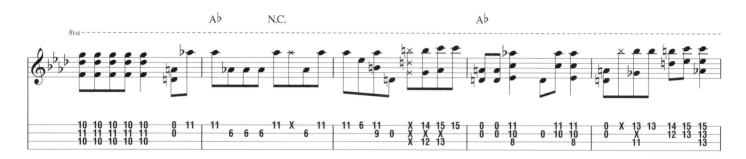

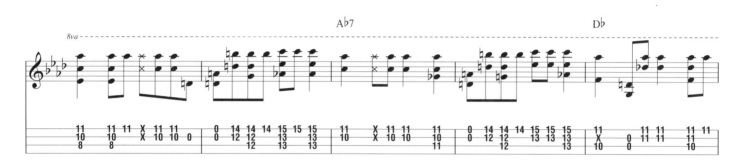

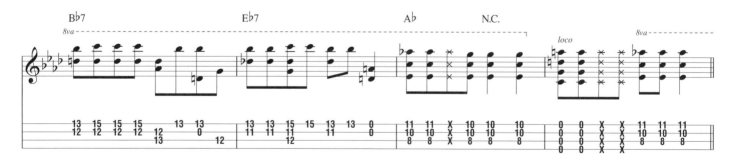

I

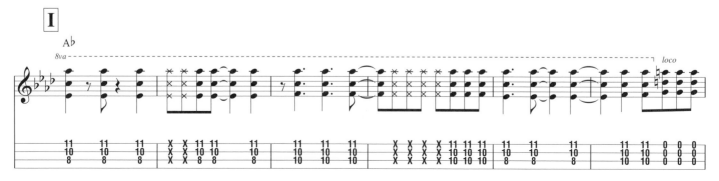

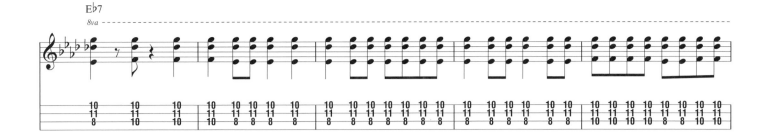

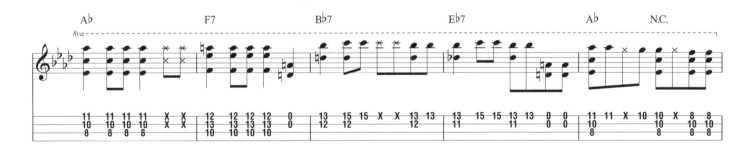

White Sandy Beach

Words and Music by Willy Dann

Uke: Low G tuning:
(low to high) G-C-E-A

Intro
Free time

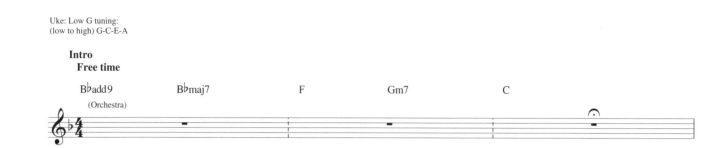

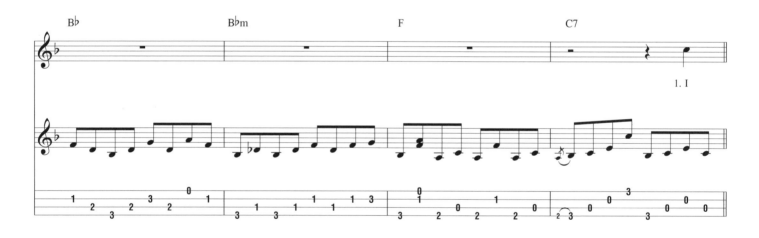

Verse

saw you in ___ my dream. ___ We were walk - ing hand _ in hand ___ on a white _

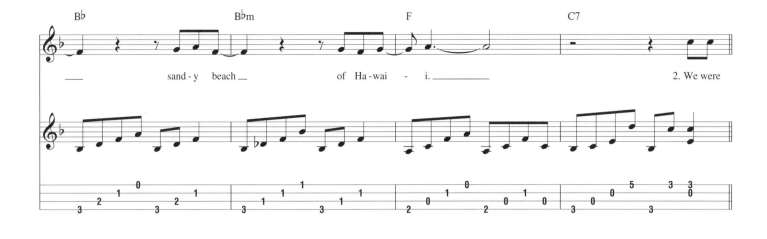

sand - y beach ___ of Ha - wai - i. _____ 2. We were

Verse

play - ing in ___ the sun. ___
hot, fun sum - mer days ___

We were hav - ing so ___ much fun ___
ly - ing there in the sun ___

on a white ___

sand - y beach ___ of Ha - wai - i. _____ The

Chorus

sound of the o - cean soothes my ___ rest - less soul.

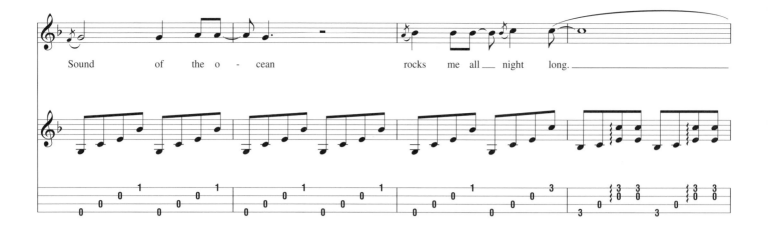

Sound of the o - cean rocks me all night long. _____

1.

2.

_____ 3. Those _____ 4. Oh, last

Verse

Uke: w/ Riff A

F

night _____ in my dreams, ___ I saw your face ___ a - gain. ___ We were there ___

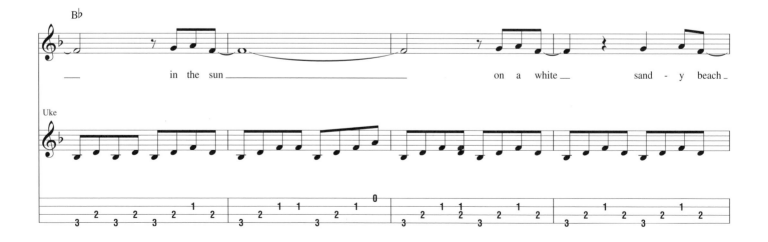

B♭

___ in the sun _____ on a white ___ sand - y beach ___

Uke

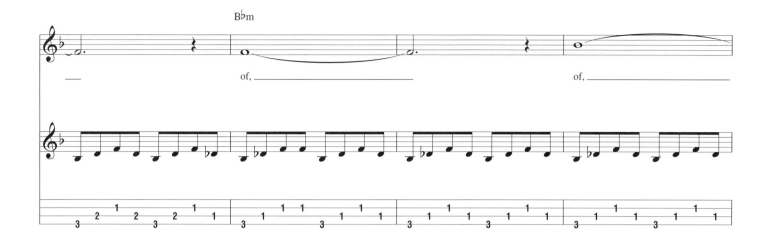

of, _____ of, _____

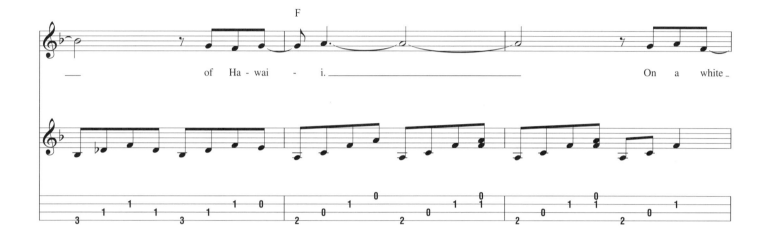

of Ha - wai - i. _____ On a white _

sand - y beach _ of Ha - wai - i. _____

Outro

F

from Eddie Vedder - *Ukulele Songs*

Tonight You Belong to Me

Words by Billy Rose
Music by Lee David

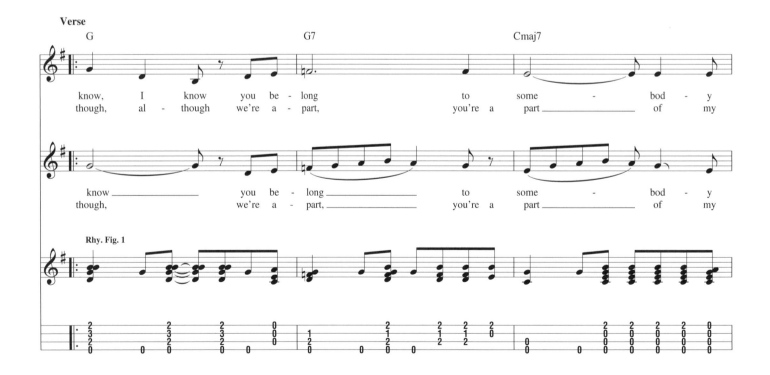

Can't Buy Me Love

Words and Music by John Lennon and Paul McCartney

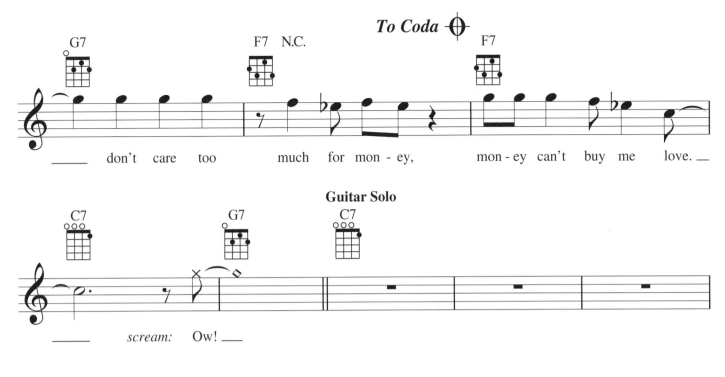

_don't care too much for mon - ey, mon - ey can't buy me love. _

Guitar Solo

_ scream: Ow! _

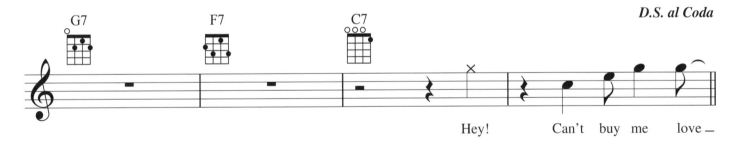

D.S. al Coda

Hey! Can't buy me love _

⊕ Coda

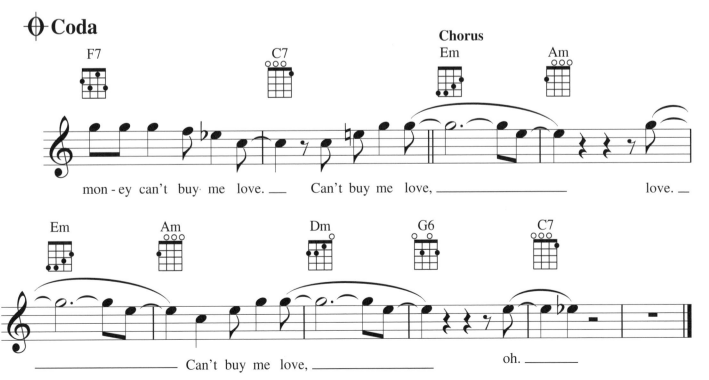

Chorus

mon - ey can't buy me love. _ Can't buy me love, _ love. _

_ Can't buy me love, _ oh. _

American Pie

Words and Music by Don McLean

with ev - 'ry pa - per I'd de - liv - er. Bad news on the door - step, I

could - n't take one more step. I can't re - mem - ber if I cried ____ when I

read a - bout ___ his wid - owed bride. ___ Some - thing touched me deep in - side, ____ the

day the mu - sic died. So,

Chorus
Moderately ♩ = 102

bye, _____ bye, Miss A - mer - i - can Pie. ___ Drove ___ my Chev - y to the lev - ee, but the

lev - ee was dry. ___ An' them good ol' ___ boys ___ were drink - in'

whis - key an' rye, ___ sing - in' "This - 'll be the day ___ that I ___ die, ___

Faster ♩ = 140

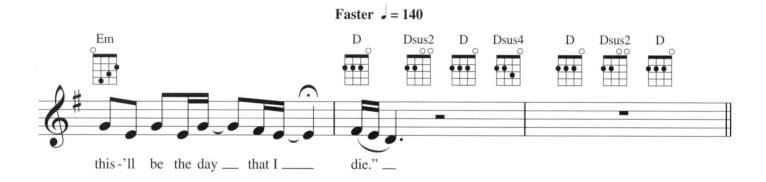

this - 'll be the day ___ that I ___ die." ___

Verse

1. Did you ___ write the book of love ___ and do you ___ have faith in
ten years ___ we've been on our own, ___ an' moss ___ grows fat on

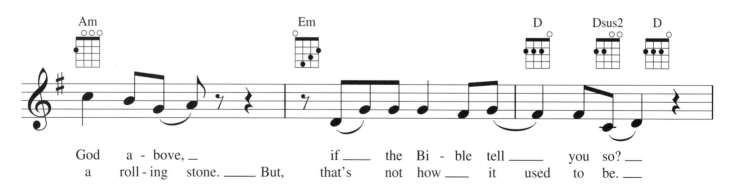

God a - bove, ___ if ___ the Bi - ble tell ___ you so? ___
a roll - ing stone. ___ But, that's not how ___ it used to be. ___

dig those rhy-thm and blues. _____ I was a lone - ly teen - age __
____ ver - dict _ was _ re - turned. _____ And while ___ Le - nin ___ read a book

bronc - in' buck __ with a pink car - na - tion an' a pick-up __ truck. _ But
____ on _ Marx, _ a quar - tet prac - ticed in the park. __ And

I knew I ____ was out _____ of luck, the day _____ the mu-
we sang _ dir - ges _____ in the dark, the day _____ the mu-

- sic died. ____ I start - ed sing - in', ___ "Bye, __
- sic died. ____ We were sing - in', ___ "Bye, __

Chorus

_____ } bye, Miss A - mer - i - can Pie. __ Drove my Chev-y to the lev - ee, but the

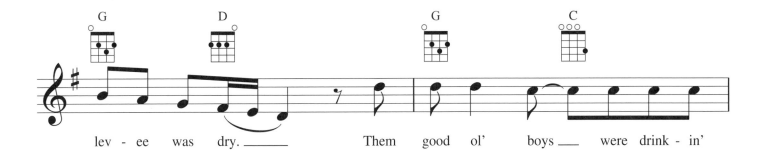

lev - ee was dry. _____ Them good ol' boys _____ were drink - in'

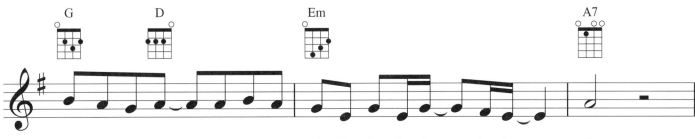

whis - key an' rye, _____ an' sing - in' this - 'll be the day _____ that I _____ die,

1.

Em   D   Dsus2 D   Dsus4 D Dsus2   D

this - 'll be the day _____ that I _____ die." _____   2. Now, _ for

2.

D   Dsus2 D   Dsus4 D   Dsus2   D   **Verse** G

die." _____   3. Hel - ter, skel - ter in
                                                 _____ there we were all

Am   C   Am

the sum - mer swelt - er. The birds _____ flew off with a fall - out shel - ter,
in one place, _ a _____ gen - er - a - tion lost in space, with

Chorus

_____ bye, Miss A - mer - i - can Pie. __ Drove my Chev - y to the lev - ee, but the

lev - ee was dry. ___ Them good ol' boys __ were drink - in' whis - key and rye, __ an' sing - in'

this -'ll be the day __ that I _____ die,   this -'ll be the day __ that I ____

1.

die." ____   4. Oh, _____ an' __ die." _____

2.

Verse
Freely

5. I met a girl who sang __ the blues __ and I asked her for some hap - py news. __   But

she just smiled _____ and turned a - way.

I went down to the sa - cred store _ where I'd heard the mu - sic years be - fore. _ But the

man there said the mu - sic would - n't play. _____ And

in the streets the chil - dren screamed. _ The lov - ers cried _ an' the po - ets dreamed. _ But

not a word was spo - ken, the church bells all were bro - ken. An' the

three men I ad - mire _ most, ___ the Fa - ther, Son and _ the Ho - ly Ghost, they

caught the last train for the coast, the day the mu - sic died.

Chorus
♩ = 102

An' they were sing - in' _____ "Bye, _____ bye, Miss A -

mer - i - can Pie. ___ Drove my Chev - y to the lev - ee, but the

lev - ee was dry. ___ An'them good ol' ___ boys ___ were drink - in'

whis - key an' rye, ___ sing - in' this - 'll be the day ___ that I ___

Outro-Chorus

49

Crazy

Words and Music by Willie Nelson

First note

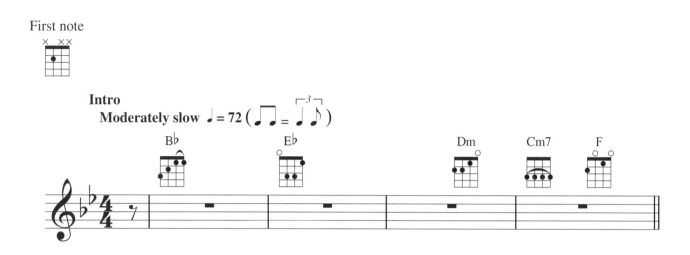

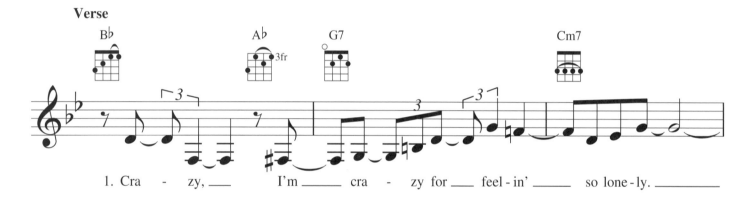

1. Cra - zy, ___ I'm ___ cra - zy for ___ feel-in' ___ so lone-ly. ___

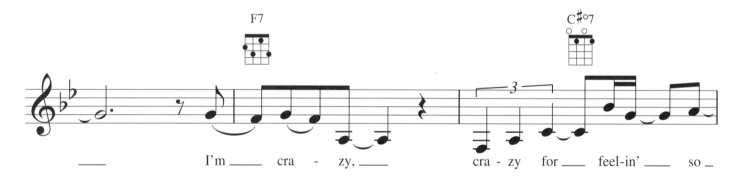

___ I'm ___ cra - zy, ___ cra - zy for ___ feel-in' ___ so

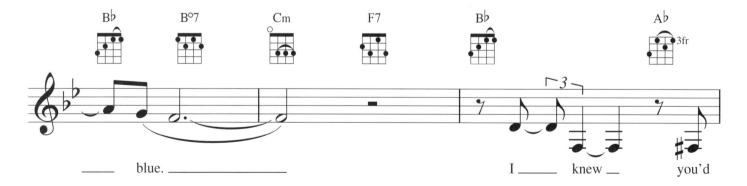

___ blue. ___ I ___ knew ___ you'd

love me as long as _____ you want - ed, _____

_____ and _____ then some - day _____ you'd

leave me for some - bod - y _____ new. _____

Bridge

Wor - ry, _____ why do I _____ let my - self wor - ry, _____

_____ won - d'rin' _____ what in the world _____ did I

51

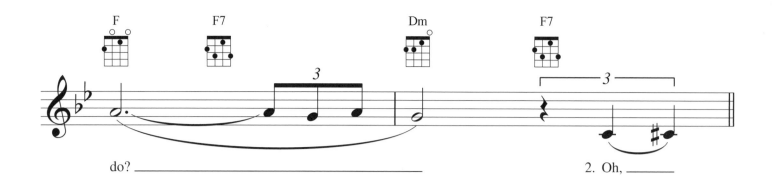

do? _____ 2. Oh, _____

Verse

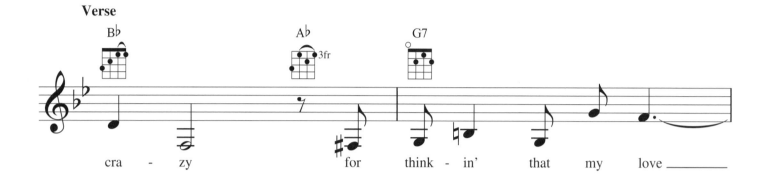

cra - zy   for   think - in'   that   my   love _____

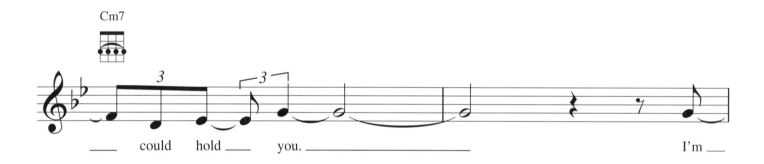

____ could   hold ____ you. _____ I'm ___

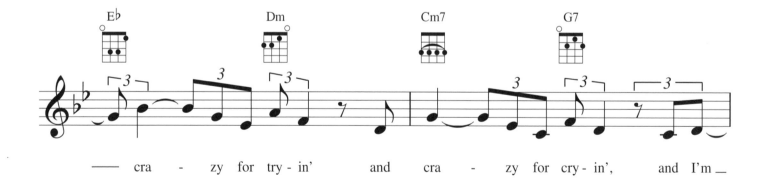

—— cra - zy for try - in'   and   cra - zy for cry - in',   and I'm__

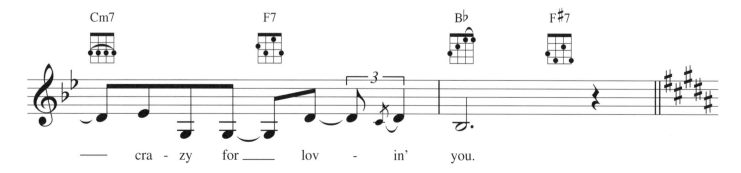

—— cra - zy   for ____ lov - in'   you.

Outro-Verse

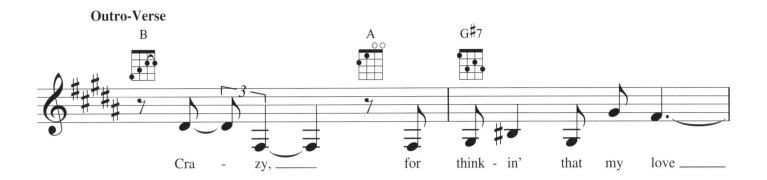

Cra - zy, _____ for think - in' that my love _____

_____ could hold _____ you. _____ I'm _____

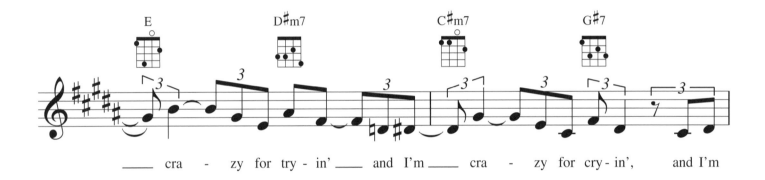

_____ cra - zy for try - in' _____ and I'm _____ cra - zy for cry - in', and I'm

cra - zy for lov - in'

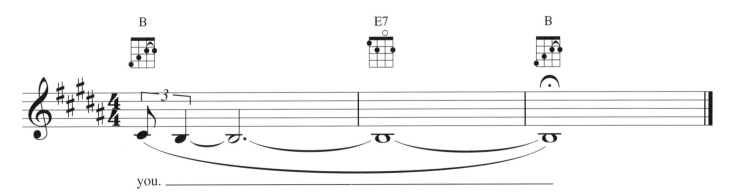

you. _____

Crocodile Rock

Words and Music by Elton John and Bernie Taupin

- gest kick I ev - er got _____ was do - ing a
- er kill the thrills we got _____ burn - ing

thing called the Croc - o - dile _____ Rock. _____ While the oth -
up to the Croc - o - dile _____ Rock. _____ Learn - ing fast _____

- er kids were rock - ing 'round the clock, we were hop -
_____ as the weeks went ___ past, _____ we real - ly

- pin' and bop - pin' to the Croc - o - dile Rock. } Well,
thought _ the Croc - o - dile _____ Rock _____ would last. }

Chorus

Croc - o - dile Rock - in' is some - thing shock - in' when your

feet just can't keep still. I nev - er knew me a

bet - ter time ___ and I guess ___ I nev - er will. ___

___ Oh, ___ lawd - y, ma - ma, those

Fri - day nights when Su - sie wore ___ her

dress - es tight ___ and the Croc - o - dile Rock - in' was a

To Coda ⊕

out _____ of - a sight. _____

Interlude

La, _____ la, la, la, la, la.

La, la, la, la, la. La, la, la, la,

1. | 2. *D.S. al Coda*

la. 2. But the years _ 3. I re - mem -

Coda
Outro

La, _____ la, la, la, la,

la. La, la, la, la, la.

Repeat and fade

La, la, la, la, la.

Cups

(When I'm Gone)

from the Motion Picture Soundtrack PITCH PERFECT

Words and Music by A.P. Carter, Luisa Gerstein
and Heloise Tunstall-Behrens

Chorus

gone,   when I'm   gone, _____ you're gon - na miss me when I'm

gone.   You're gon - na   miss   me   by   my   hair, _____ you'll
                                                           walk, _____ you're gon - na

miss me ev - 'ry - where. _ Oh,   you're gon - na miss me when I'm
miss me by my talk. ___

gone.   When I'm   gone,   when I'm   gone, _____

you're gon - na miss me when I'm   gone.   You're gon - na

miss me by my   walk, _ you're gon - na   miss   me   by   my   talk. _ Oh, _
hair, _ you're gon - na   miss   me   ev - 'ry - where. _ Oh, you're

59

you're gon - na miss me when I'm gone.
sure gon - na miss me when I'm

Interlude

2nd time, D.S. al Coda

N.C.(C)

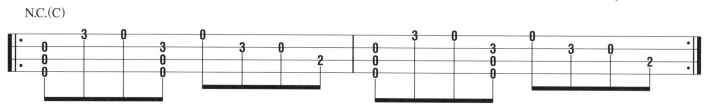

⊕ **Coda**

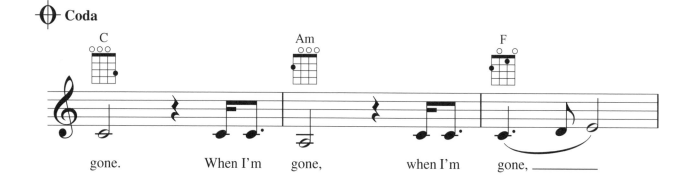

gone. When I'm gone, when I'm gone, _____

you're gon - na miss me when I'm gone. You're gon - na

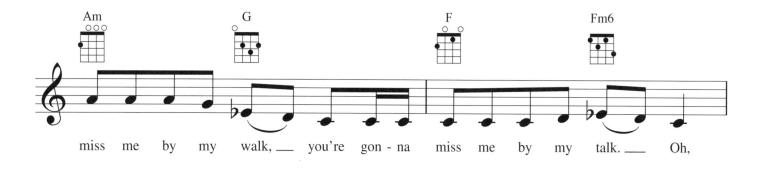

miss me by my walk, ___ you're gon - na miss me by my talk. ___ Oh,

you're gon - na miss me when I'm gone.

Don't Cry for Me Argentina

from EVITA
Words by Tim Rice
Music by Andrew Lloyd Webber

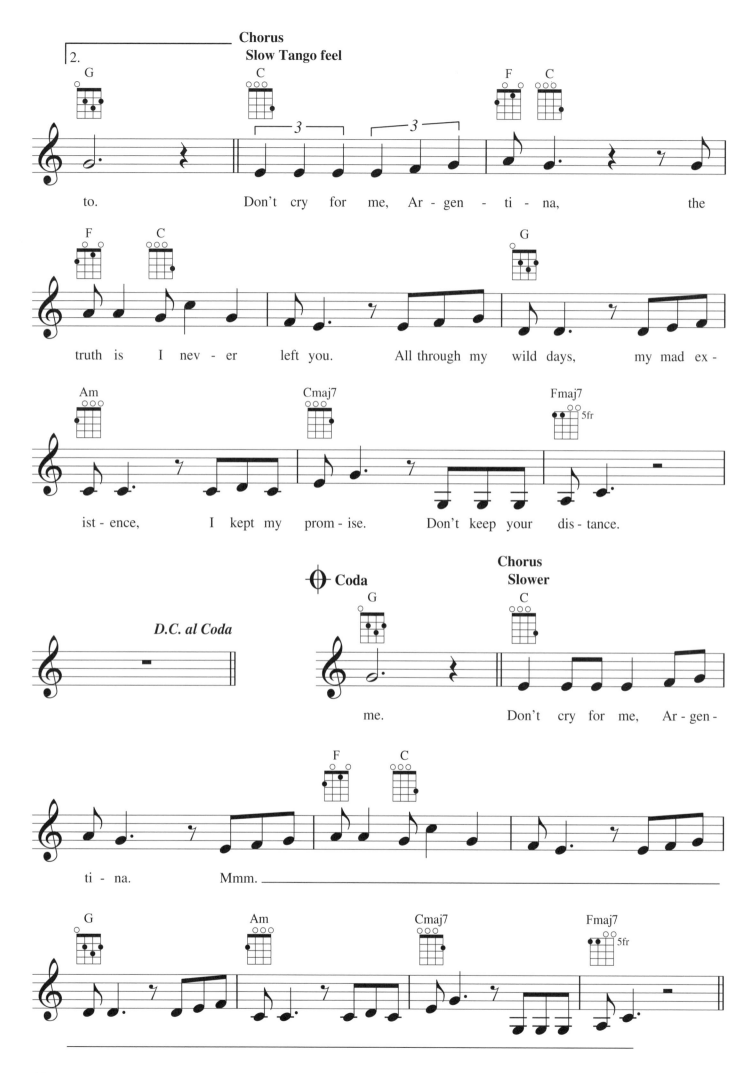

Additional Lyrics

2. I had to let it happen, I had to change;
   Couldn't stay all my life down at heel,
   Looking out of the window, staying out of the sun.
   So I chose freedom, running around trying everything new,
   But nothing impressed me at all. I never expected it to.

3. And as for fortune and as for fame,
   I never invited them in,
   Though it seemed to the world they were all I desired.
   They are illusions, they're not the solutions they promised to be.
   The answer was here all the time. I love you and hope you love me.

Day-O
(The Banana Boat Song)

Words and Music by Irving Burgie and William Attaway

First note

Intro
Moderate Calypso ♩ = 122

N.C.

Day - light come ___ and me wan' go home. ___

Verse

C

1. Work all night ___ on a drink of rum. ___

Day - light come ___ and me wan' go home.

Stack ba - nan - a till de morn - ing come. ___

Day - light come ___ and me wan' go home.

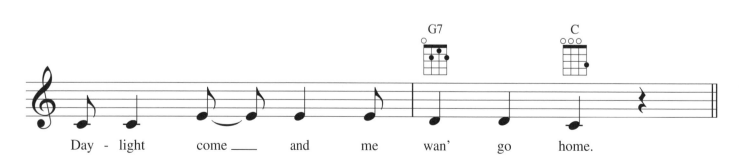

Day - light come ____ and me wan' go home.
Day - light come ____ and me wan' go home.

Six - hand, sev - en hand, eight - hand bunch.
Hide the dead - ly black ta - ran - t'la.

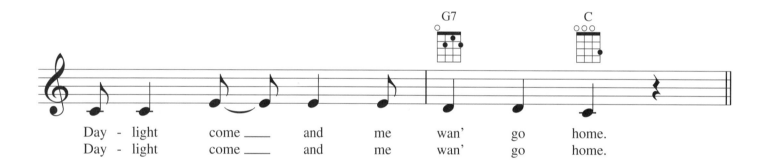

Day - light come ____ and me wan' go home.
Day - light come ____ and me wan' go home.

Chorus

Day, me say day - o. ____ Day - light come __ and me

wan' go home. Day, me say day, me say day, me say...

Five Foot Two, Eyes of Blue
(Has Anybody Seen My Girl?)

Words by Joe Young and Sam Lewis
Music by Ray Henderson

1., 3. Five foot two, eyes of blue, but oh what those five
2., 4. Turned up nose, turned down hose, nev - er had no

foot could do. ____
oth - er beaus. ____ } Has an - y - bod - y seen my

girl? ____

seen my

girl? ____ Now if you run in - to a

five foot two, cov - ered with fur, ____

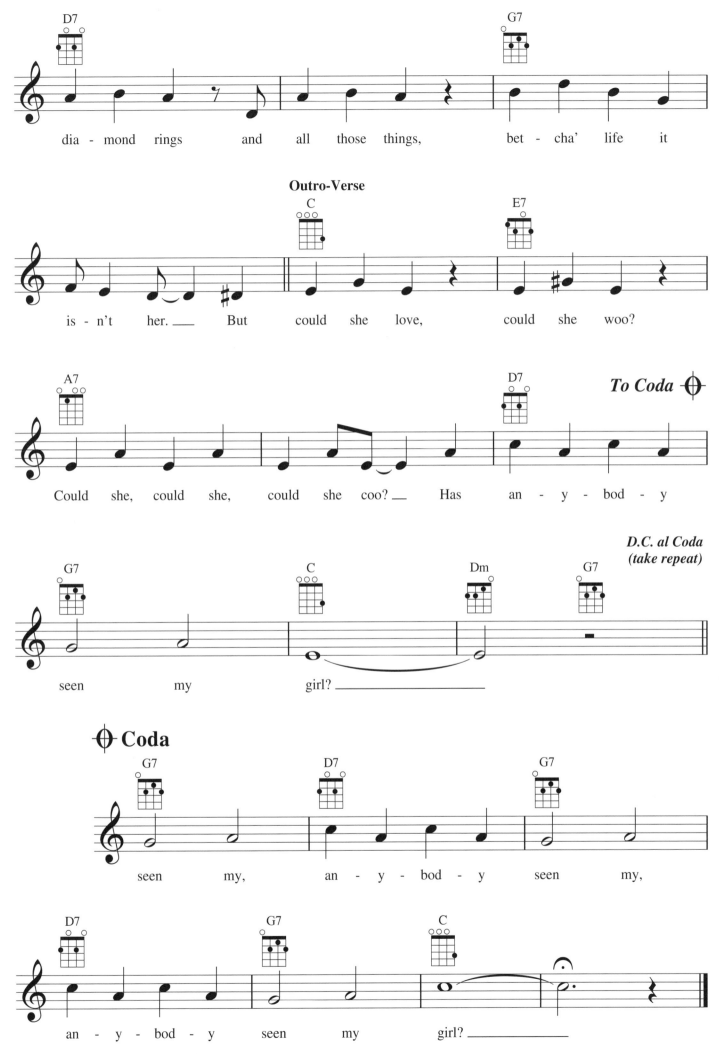

dia - mond rings and all those things, bet - cha' life it

Outro-Verse

is - n't her. ___ But could she love, could she woo?

Could she, could she, could she coo? ___ Has an - y - bod - y

To Coda ⊕

D.C. al Coda
(take repeat)

seen my girl? _____

⊕ **Coda**

seen my, an - y - bod - y seen my,

an - y - bod - y seen my girl? _____

How Sweet It Is
(To Be Loved by You)

Words and Music by Edward Holland, Lamont Dozier and Brian Holland

and thank you, ba - by. I wan - na stop, ___

_____

and thank you, ba - by.

Chorus

How sweet it is ___ to be ___ loved ___ by

you. ___ Yes, it is, ba - by.

How sweet it is ___ to be ___ loved ___ by

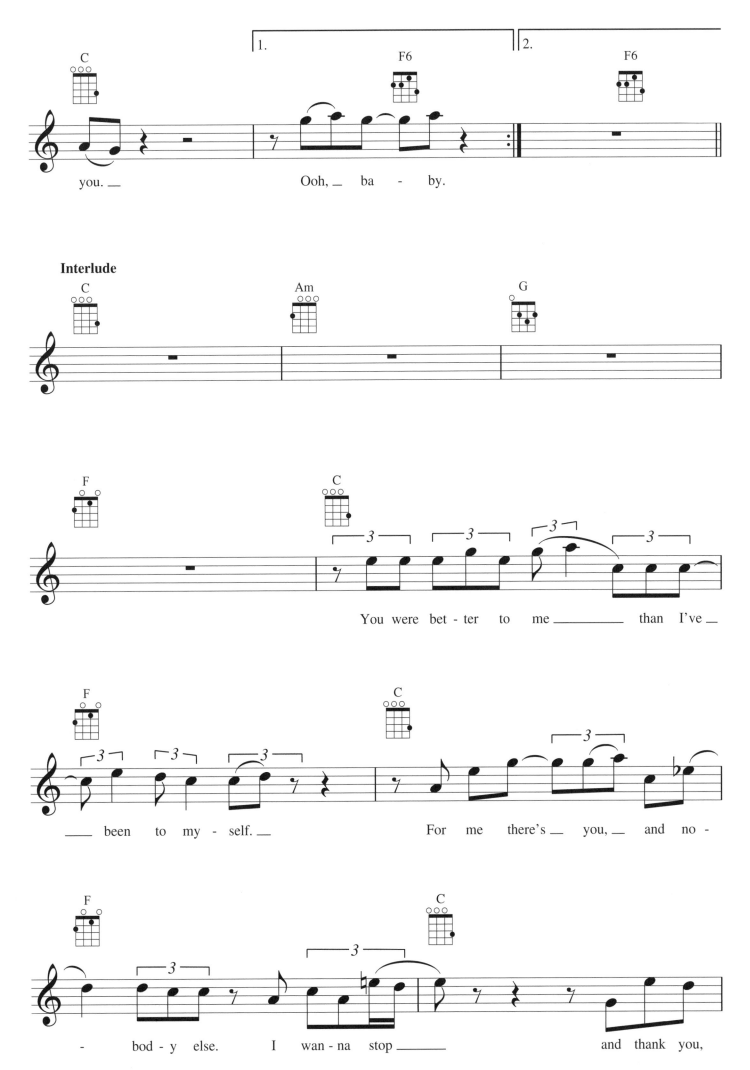

you. __   Ooh, __ ba - by.

Interlude

You were bet - ter to me _____ than I've __ _____ been to my - self. __   For me there's __ you, __ and no - - bod - y else.   I wan - na stop _____   and thank you,

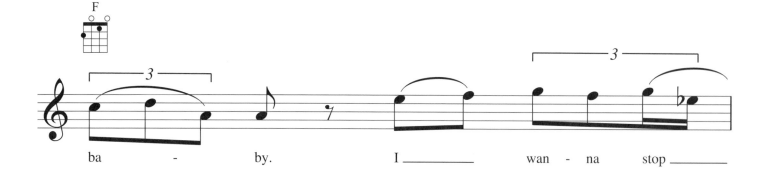

ba - by.   I _____ wan - na stop _____

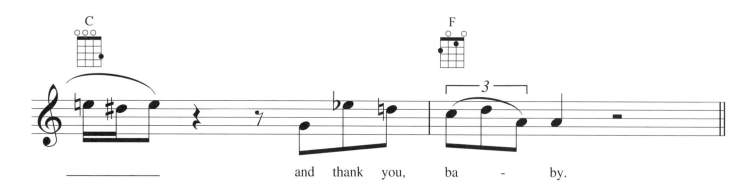

_____   and thank you, ba - by.

Chorus

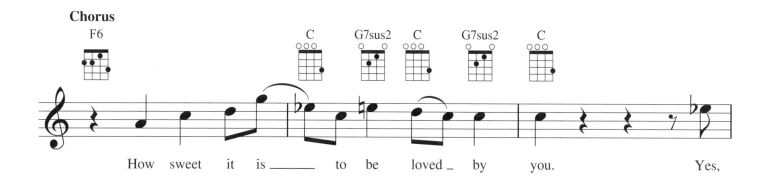

How sweet it is _____ to be loved _ by you.   Yes,

Begin fade

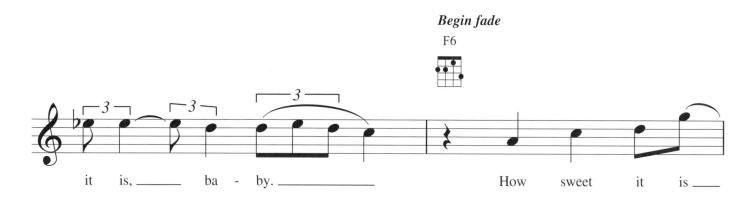

it is, _____ ba - by. _____   How sweet it is ___

Fade out

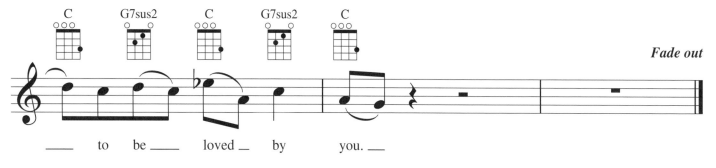

___ to be ___ loved _ by you. ___

74

I Will Follow You Into the Dark

Words and Music by Benjamin Gibbard

Bb

_____ but I'll be close be-hind.   I'll fol-low you _____
_____ I got my knuck-les _____ bruised   by a la -
_____ from Bang-kok to Cal - ga - ry,   and the soles _____

F   C   F

_____ in - to the dark. _____   No blind - ing _____ light _____
- dy in black. _____   And I held my _____ tongue _
_____ of your shoes _____   are all worn _____ down. _

Dm

_____ or tun-nels to gates of _____ white, _____   just our hands
_____ as _____ she told me, _____ "Son, _____   fear is the
_____ The time _ for sleep is _ now, _____   but it's noth-ing to

Bb   F   *3rd time, To Coda 1* ⊕

clasped so _____ tight _____   wait-ing for _____   3   the hint of a
heart of _____ love." _____   So I nev -   er went back. _
cry a - bout   'cause we'll hold _____   each oth - er   soon _

𝄋 𝄋 **Chorus**

C   Dm   F

                    3
spark.   If heav - en and hell de - cide _____   that they both _

Bb   F   C   Dm

_____ are sat - is - fied, _____   il - lum - i - nate _ the no's _

on their va - can - cy signs. ____ If

there's no one be - side ____ you when your soul ____ em - barks, ____

____ then I'll fol - low you ____ in - to the dark.

To Coda 2 1. 2. *D.S. al Coda 1*

2. In

Coda 1

____ in the black - est ____ of rooms. ____

D.S.S. al Coda 2 **Coda 2**

____ If

And

rit.

I'll fol - low you ____ in - to the dark.

Is You Is, Or Is You Ain't
(Ma' Baby)

from FIVE GUYS NAMED MOE

**Words and Music by Billy Austin
and Louis Jordan**

when you're sure of one, you find {she's / he's} gone and made a change. __

Chorus

__ Is you is, or is you ain't ma' ba-

- by? May - be ba - by's

found some - bod - y new, _____ or

1.

is ma' ba - by still ma' ba - by true? ___

2.

still ma' ba - by true? _____

80

Mean

Words and Music by Taylor Swift

First note

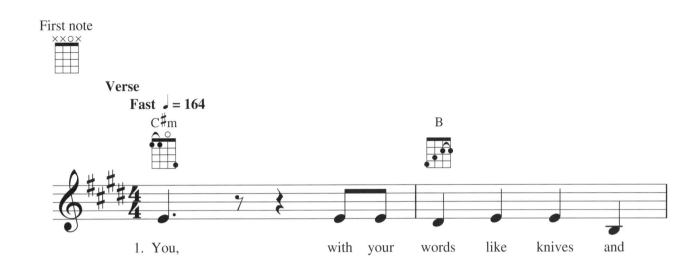

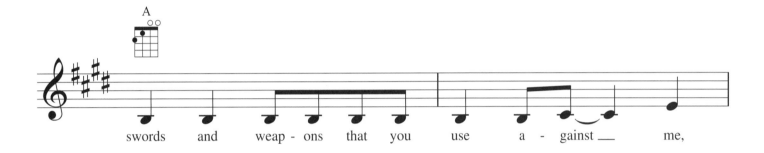

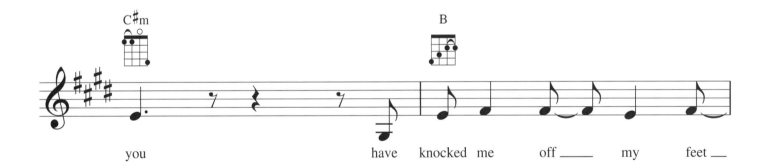

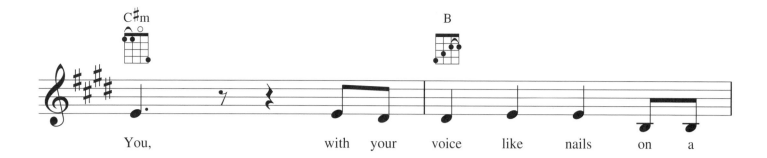

You, with your voice like nails on a

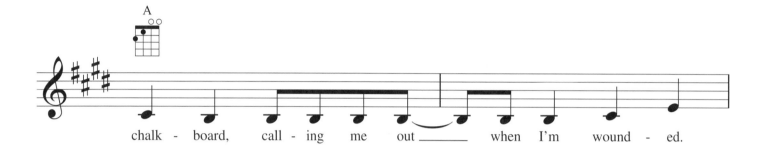

chalk - board, call - ing me out _____ when I'm wound - ed.

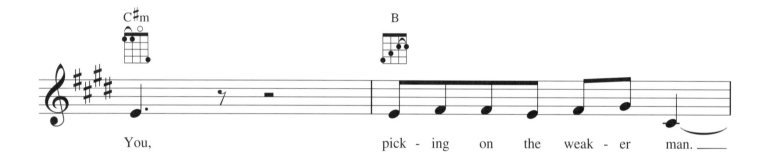

You, pick - ing on the weak - er man. _____

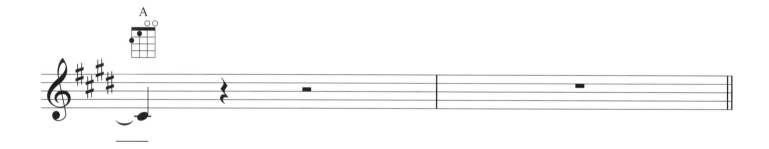

Pre-Chorus

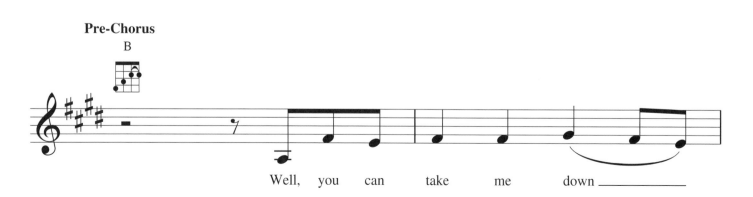

Well, you can take me down _____

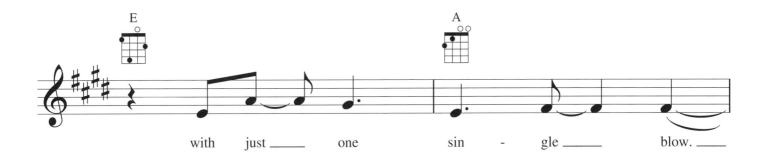

with   just ____   one   sin - gle ____   blow. ____

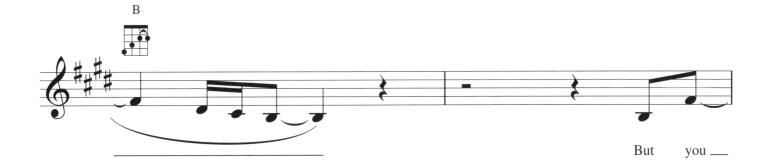

_____   But   you ____

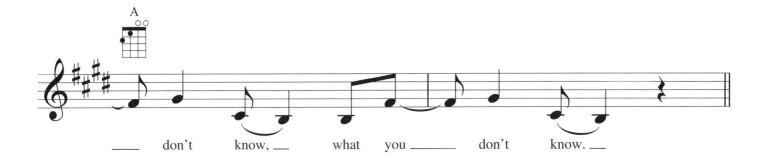

____   don't   know, ____   what   you ____   don't   know. ____

𝄋 Chorus

Some - day, ____   I'll   be

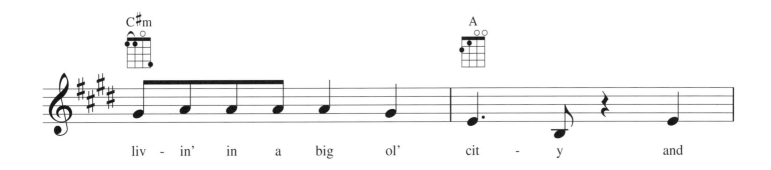

liv - in'   in   a   big   ol'   cit - y   and

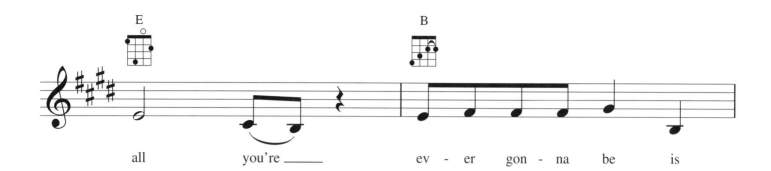

all you're _____ ev - er gon - na be is

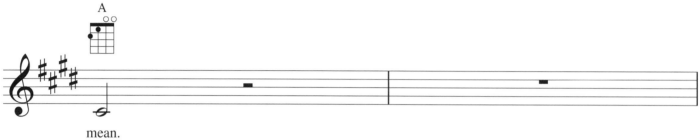

mean.

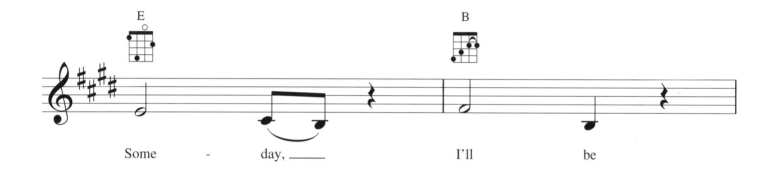

Some - day, _____ I'll be

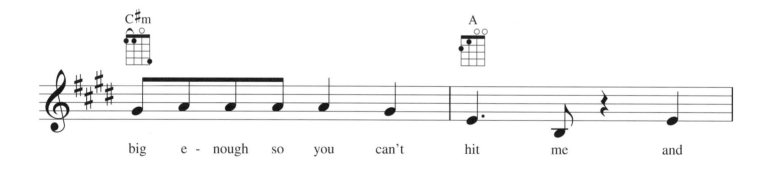

big e - nough so you can't hit me and

To Coda ⊕

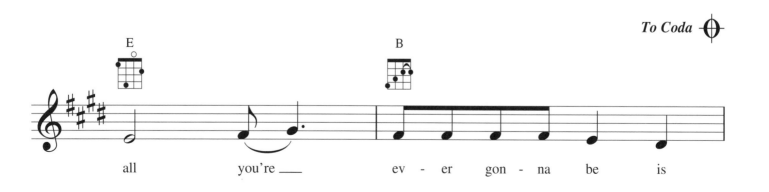

all you're _____ ev - er gon - na be is

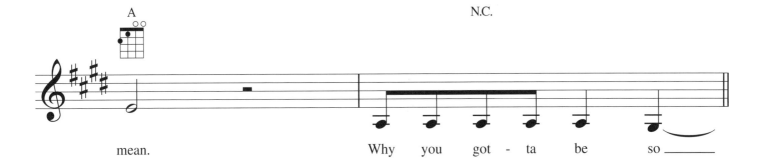

mean.

Why you got - ta be so _____

Interlude

_____ mean?

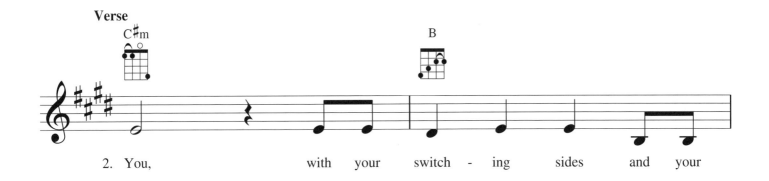

Verse

2. You,   with your switch - ing sides and your

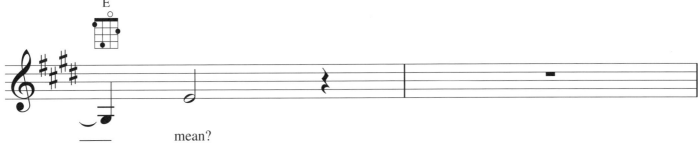

wild - fire lies and your hu - mil - i - a - tion,

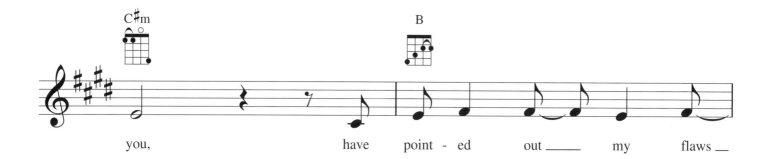

you,   have point - ed out _____ my flaws _____

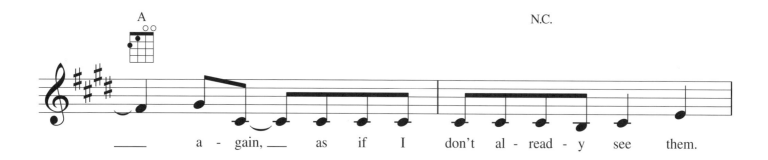

_____ a - gain, ___ as if I don't al - read - y see them.

I walk with my _____ head down, ___ tryin' to

block you out 'cause I'll nev - er im - press you.

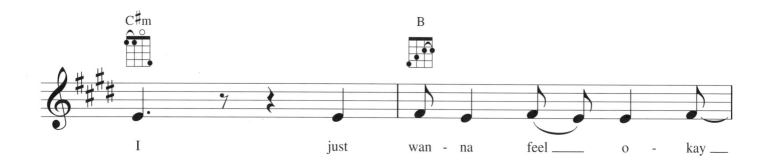

I just wan - na feel ___ o - kay ___

a - gain. ___

Pre-Chorus

I bet you got pushed a - round, _____

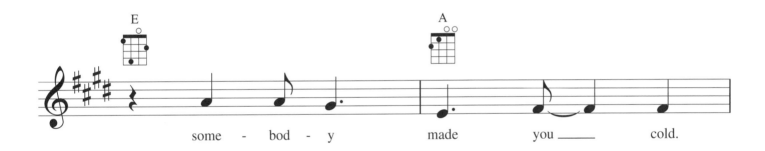

some - bod - y made you ___ cold.

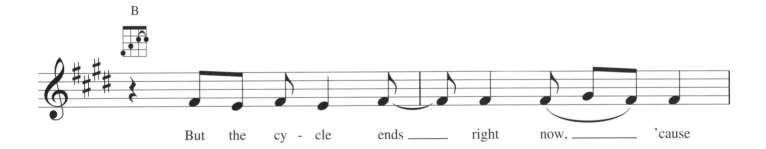

But the cy - cle ends ___ right now, _____ 'cause

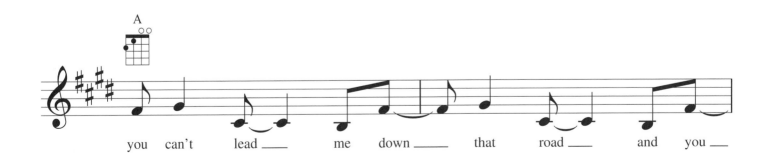

you can't lead ___ me down ___ that road ___ and you ___

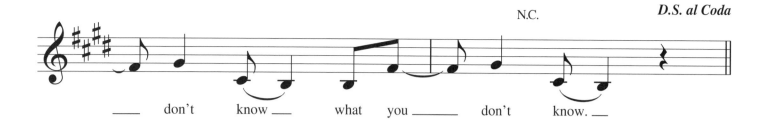

N.C.

_____ don't know _____ what you _____ don't know. _____

Coda

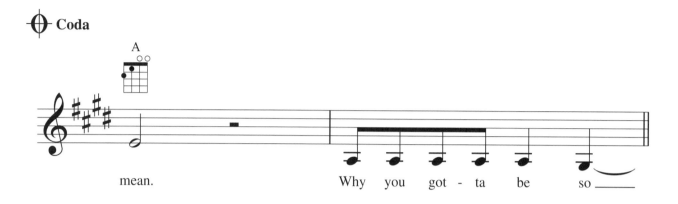

A

mean.

Why you got - ta be so _____

Interlude

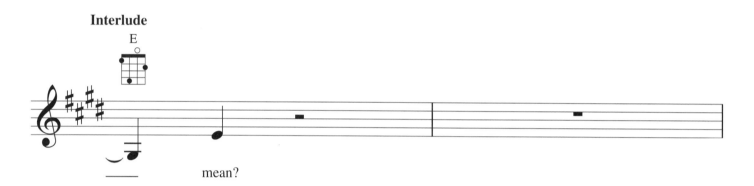

E

_____ mean?

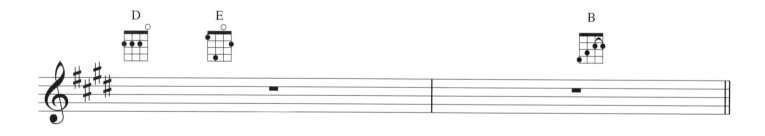

D   E   B

Mandolin Solo

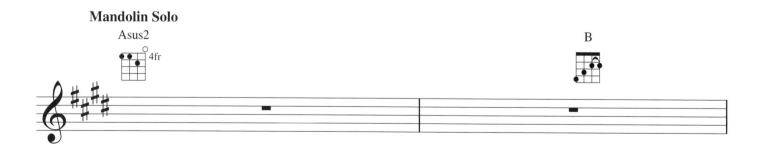

Asus2   B
4fr

And I can _____

Bridge

see you years ___ from now _____ in a bar, _____

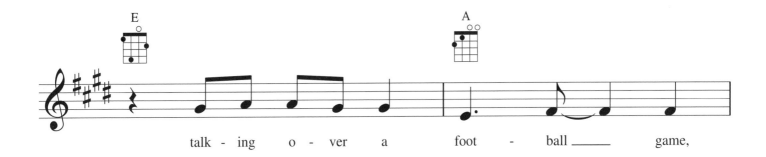

talk - ing o - ver a foot - ball _____ game,

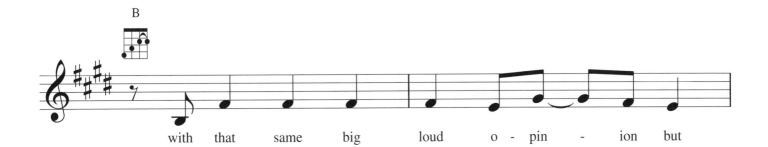

with that same big loud o - pin - ion but

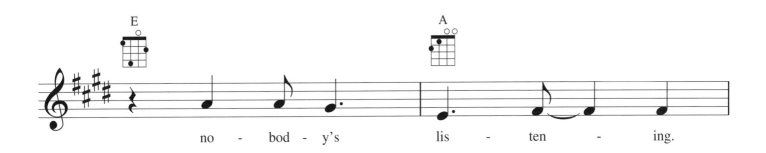

no - bod - y's lis - ten - ing.

Washed up and rant - ing a - bout the same old

bit - ter things.

Drunk and grum - blin' on _____ a - bout _____ how

I ____ can't sing. But all you are is ____

Interlude

____ mean.

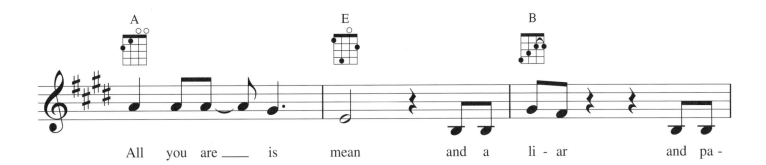

All you are ___ is mean and a li - ar and pa -

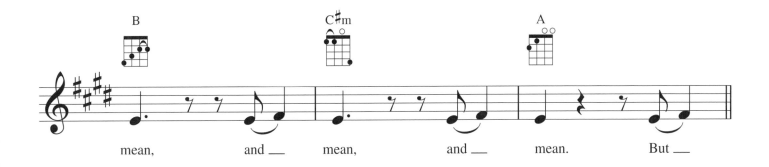

thet - ic and a - lone in life ___ and mean, and ___

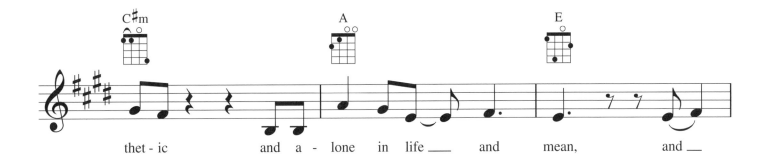

mean, and ___ mean, and ___ mean. But ___

Chorus

N.C.

some - day, ___ I'll be liv - in' in a big ol'

cit - y and all you're ___ ev - er gon - na be is

mean.   Yeah! _____ Some - day, __

I'll __ be big e - nough so you can't hit me and

all you're __ ev - er gon - na be is

Chorus

mean.   Some - day, __

I'll be liv - in' in a big ol' cit - y and

all you're _____ ev - er gon - na be is

mean. Some - day, ___

I'll ___ be big e - nough so you can't hit me and

all you're _____ ev - er gon - na be is mean.

Why you got - ta be so _____ mean?

The Lazy Song

Words and Music by Bruno Mars, Ari Levine, Philip Lawrence and Keinan Warsame

turn the T - V on, throw my hand in my pants. _____
real - ly nice girl, have some real - ly nice sex, and

No - bod - y's gon' tell me I can't, _____ no. I'll be
she's gon - na scream out, "This is great." _____ *Spoken: (Oh my god, this is great.)* Yeah, I

loung - in' on the couch, just chill - in' in my Snug - gie,
might mess a - round and get my col - lege de - gree. I

click to M - T - V so they can teach me how to doug - ie, 'cause
bet my old man will be so proud of me. Well,

in my cas - tle, I'm the frick - in' _____ man. _____
sor - ry, Pops, you'll just have to wait. _____ Oh, _____

Pre-Chorus

yes, I said it, I said it, I said it 'cause _ I can. _ To -

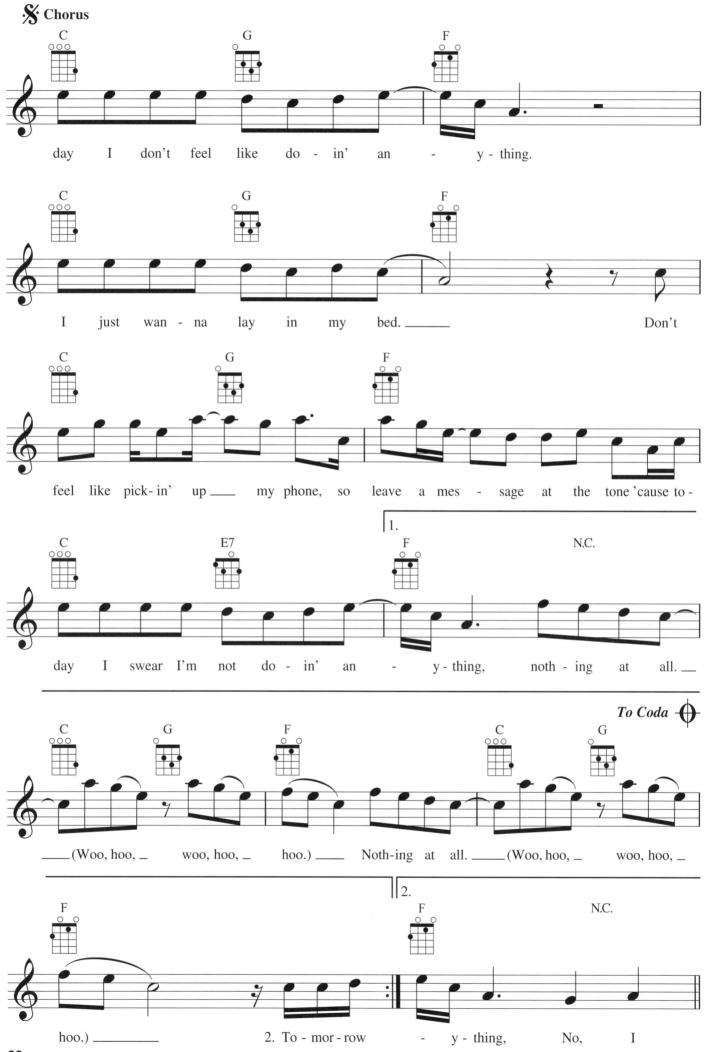

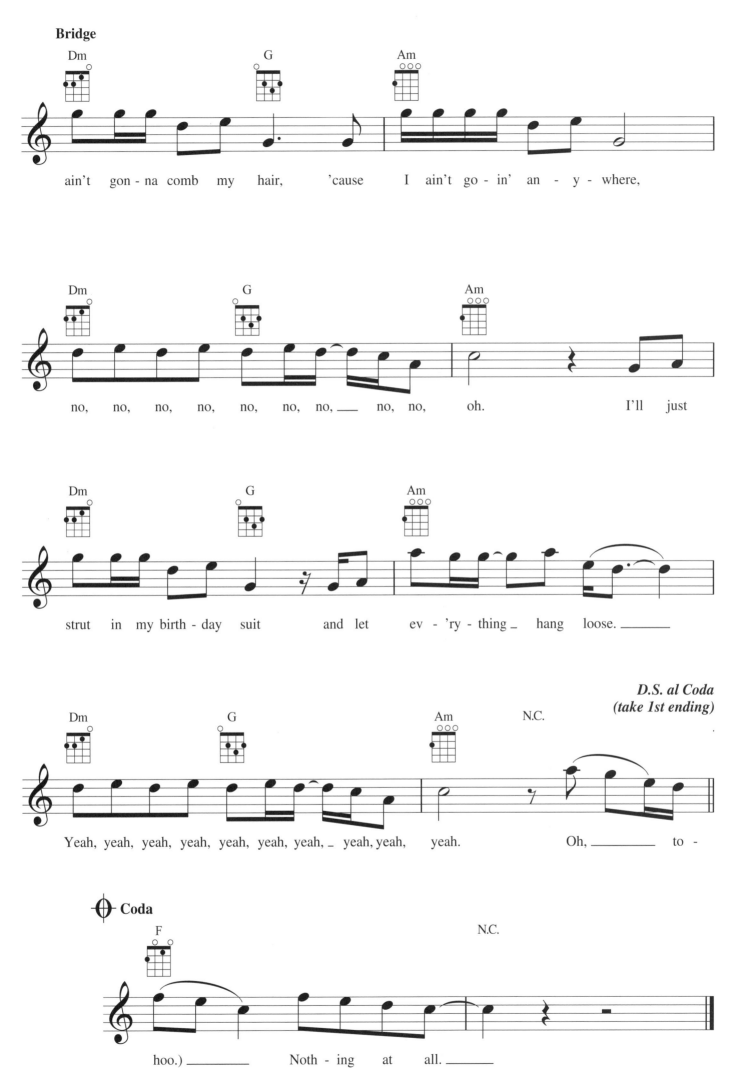

Bridge

ain't gon - na comb my hair, 'cause I ain't go - in' an - y - where,

no, no, no, no, no, no, no, ___ no, no, oh. I'll just

strut in my birth - day suit and let ev - 'ry - thing _ hang loose. ___

D.S. al Coda
(take 1st ending)

Yeah, yeah, yeah, yeah, yeah, yeah, yeah, _ yeah, yeah, yeah. Oh, ___ to -

Coda

hoo.) ___ Noth - ing at all. ___

Lucky

Words and Music by Jason Mraz, Colbie Caillat and Timothy Fagan

Chorus

Bridge

love   like   this.   Ev - 'ry   time   we   say   good - bye,

I   wish   we   had   one   more   kiss.   I'll   wait   for   you,   I

prom - ise   you   I   will. _____   I'm _____

𝄋𝄋 **Chorus**

_____   luck - y   I'm   in _____   love   with   my   best   friend,   luck - y   to   have ___
Both: Luck - y

_____   been   where   I   have   been.   Luck - y   to   be   com - ing   home   a -

- gain. _____   Luck - y   we're   in ___

100

___ love in ev - 'ry   way,   luck - y to have ___ stayed where we have

To Coda 2

stayed.   Luck - y to be com - ing   home some - day. _____

D.S. al Coda 1   **Coda 1**   *D.S.S. al Coda 2*

___   *Male:* 2. And   so   I'm   here,   right   now.

Coda 2   **Outro**

___   Oo, _____

1.

___   oo.

2.

oo, _____   oo. _____

Pearly Shells
(Pupu `O `Ewa)

Words and Music by Webley Edwards and Leon Pober

Red Sails in the Sunset

Words by Jimmy Kennedy
Music by Hugh Williams (Will Grosz)

Rocky Top

Words and Music by Boudleaux Bryant and Felice Bryant

First note

Verse
Country Two-step

1. Wish that I was on ol' Rock - y Top,
3. Once two stran - gers climbed ol' Rock - y Top,

down in the Ten - nes - see hills.
look - in' for a moon - shine still.

Ain't no smog - gy smoke on Rock - y Top,
Stran - gers ain't come down from Rock - y Top,

ain't no tel - e - phone _____ bills.
reck - on they nev - er _____ will.

me. Good ol' Rock - y Top,

Rock - y Top, Ten - nes - see,

To Coda 1. 2. *D.S. al Coda*

Rock - y Top, Ten - nes - see. see.

Coda

see. Rock - y Top, Ten - nes -

see.

Route 66

By Bobby Troup

two thou - sand miles ___ all the way. ___ Get your

kicks on Route Six - ty - six. ___ Now you

Bridge

go through Saint Loo - ey, Jop - lin, Mis - sou - ri and Ok - la - ho - ma Cit - y looks

might - y ___ pret - ty. You'll see Am - a - ril - lo, Gal - lup, New

Mex - i - co; ___ Flag - staff, Ar - i - zo - na, don't ___ for - get Wi - no - na, King -

- man, Bar - stow, San Ber - nar - di - no. 3. Won't ___ you get hip ___

___ to this time - ly tip, ___ when you make that

Cal - i - for - nia trip? ___ Get your kicks on

Interlude

Route Six - ty - six. ___

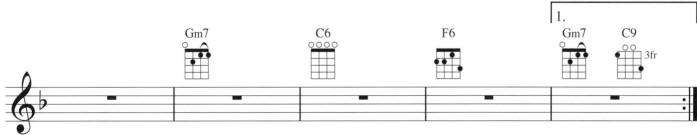

Outro

113

Sunny

Words and Music by Bobby Hebb

My sun - ny one ___ shines so sin - cere. Sun - ny one so
now I feel ___ ten feet tall. ___ Sun - ny one so

1.

true, I love you. ___

2.

true, I love you. ___

Verse

3. Sun - ny, thank you for the truth you've let me see. ___

___ Sun - ny, thank you for the

facts from __ A to Z. ____ My life was torn __ like

wind-blown sand, _ then a rock was formed when we held hands. _

Sun-ny one so true, I love ___ you. _

Verse

4. Sun - ny, thank you for that smile _ up - on your _ face, _

___ mm. ___ Sun - ny, thank you, thank you for

that gleam that flows with grace. ___ You're my spark of

na - ture's ___ fire; ___ you're my sweet com - plete de - sire. ___

Sun - ny one ___ so true, _____ yes, I love ___ you. _____

Verse

5. Sun - ny, _____ yes - ter - day all my

Repeat and fade

Sweet Home Chicago

Words and Music by Robert Johnson

Unchained Melody

from the Motion Picture UNCHAINED

Lyric by Hy Zaret
Music by Alex North

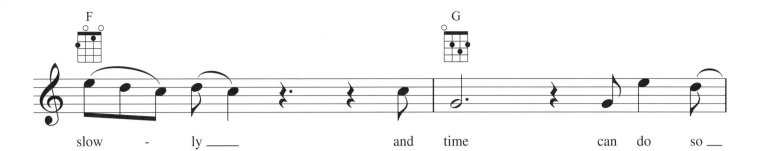

slow - ly _____ and time can do so _____

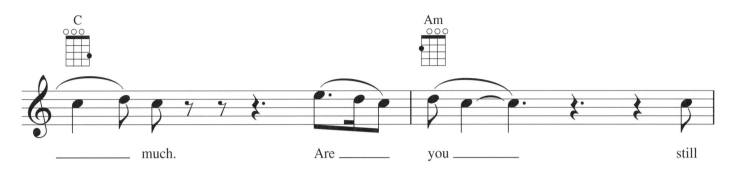

_____ much. Are _____ you _____ still

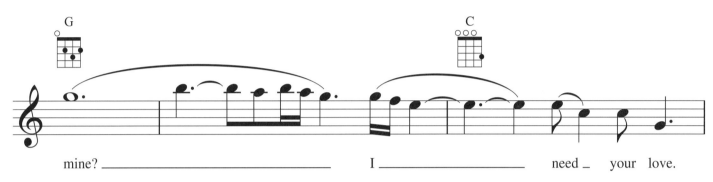

mine? _____ I _____ need _ your love.

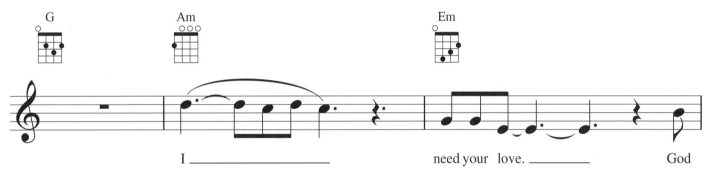

I _____ need your love. _____ God

To Coda ✆

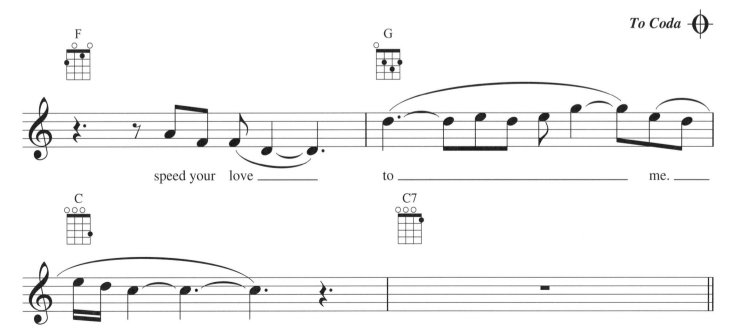

speed your love _____ to _____ me. _____

Bridge

Lone - ly _____ riv - ers flow to the sea, to the sea,

to the _____ o - pen arms _____ of the sea, _____ yeah. _____

Lone - ly _____ riv - ers sigh, "Wait for me, _____ wait for me.

D.C. al Coda

I'll be _____ com - ing home. Wait for me!" _____

Coda

Use Somebody

Words and Music by Caleb Followill, Nathan Followill, Jared Followill and Matthew Followill

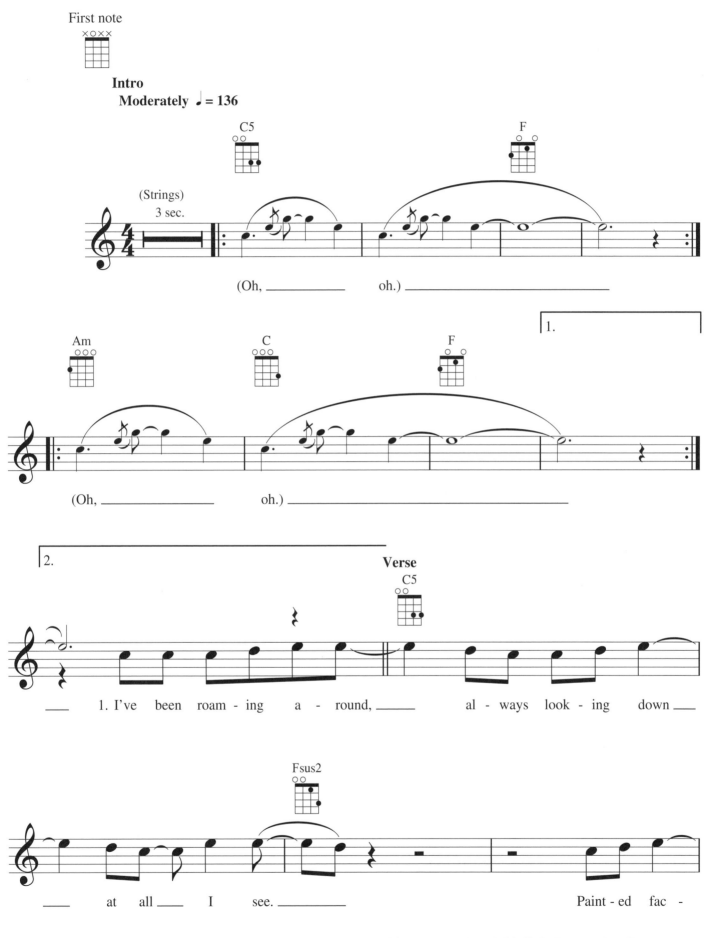

- es fill the plac - es I ___ can't reach. ___

You know __ that I could use some - bod - y. ___

You know _ that I could use some - bod - y, ___

𝄋 Verse

some - one __ like you. ___ 2. And all __ you know __ and how _ you speak. _
__ while you live it up ____ I'm off __ to sleep __

____ Count - less lov - ers un - der cov -
____ wag - ing wars ____ to shake the po -

- er of __ the street. ___ You know _ that I could
- et and _ the beat. ___ I hope _ it's gon - na

126

*Upstem note sung 1st time only.

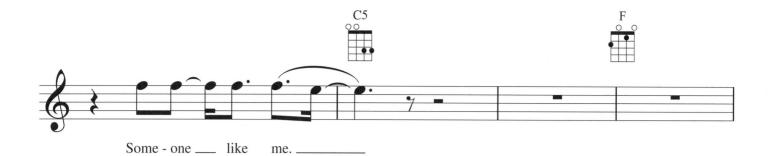

Some - one ___ like   me. _____

Some - one ___ like   me, _____ some - bod - y. _____

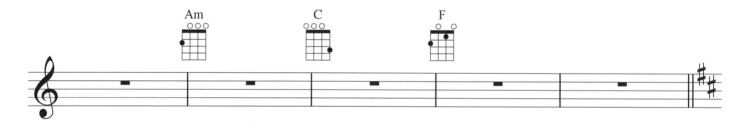

Bridge

(Oh, _ let it out.   Oh, _ let it out.   Oh, _ let it out.   Oh, _

let it out.   Oh, _ let it out.   Oh, _ let it out.   Oh, _ let it out.)

Interlude

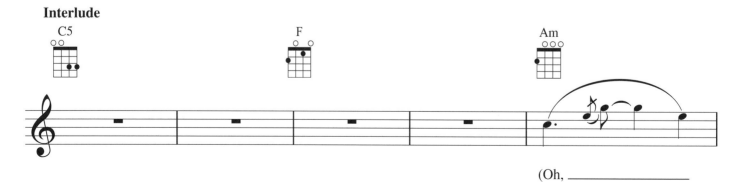

(Oh, _____

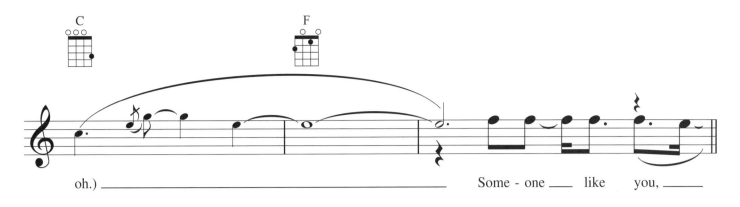

oh.) _____ Some - one __ like you, __

Chorus

Cont. bkgd. voc. fig., next 12 meas.

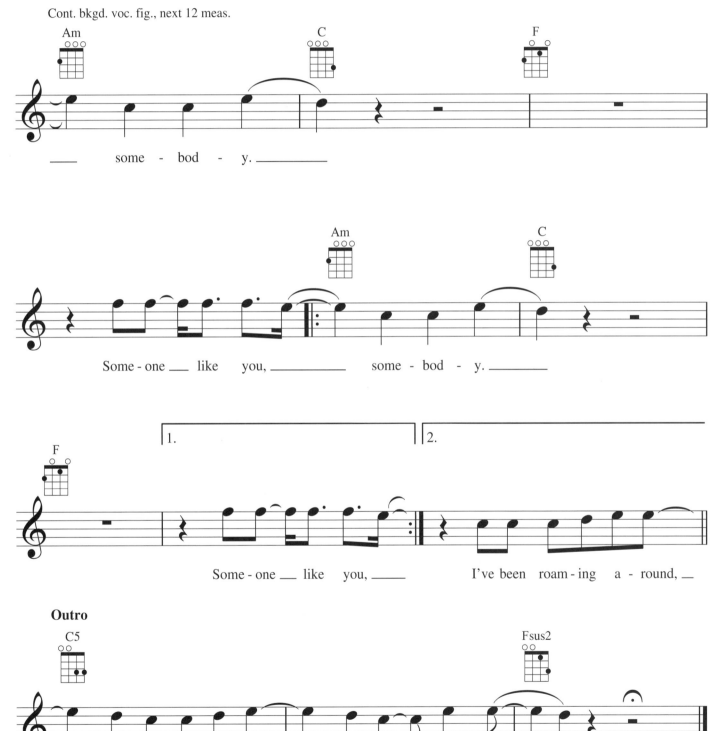

__ some - bod - y. _____

Some - one __ like you, _____ some - bod - y. _____

1.

2.

Some - one __ like you, ___ I've been roam - ing a - round, _

Outro

__ al - ways look - ing down ___ at all __ I see. _____

Under the Sea

from Walt Disney's THE LITTLE MERMAID

Music by Alan Menken
Lyrics by Howard Ashman

Bridge

_____ play   the flute. The carp _____ play   the harp. The plaice ____ play   the bass, and they _

_____ sound - in' sharp. The bass _____ play the brass. The chub ____ play the tub.   The fluke _

_____ is   the duke   of   soul.   The ray, _____ he   can play. The ling's _

_____ on   the strings. The trout ____ rock - in' out. The black - fish, she stings.   The smelt _

_____ and   the sprat, they know ____ where it's at.   And   oh,   that   blow - fish

Interlude

blow.

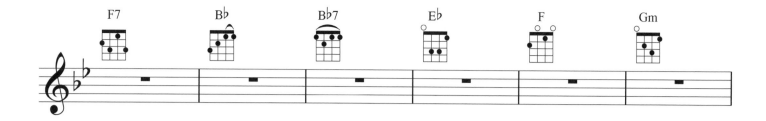

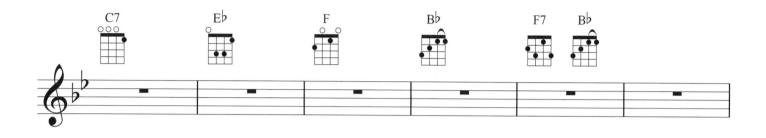

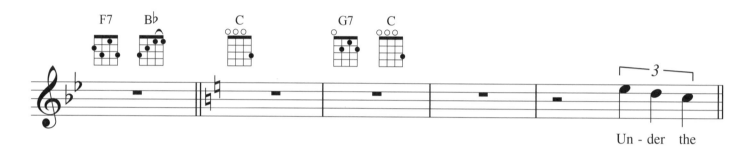

Un - der the

Chorus

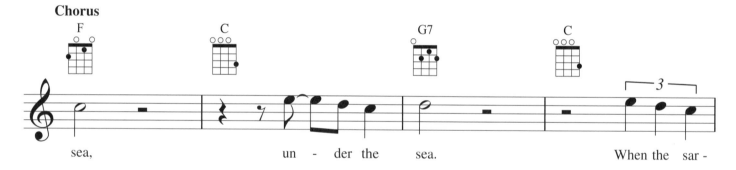

sea,   un - der the   sea.   When the sar -

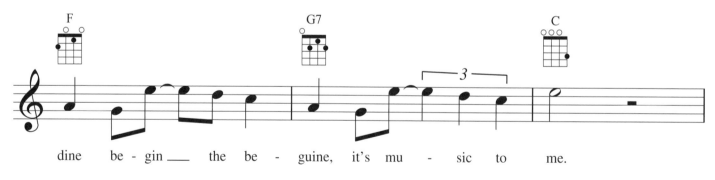

dine be - gin ___ the be - guine, it's mu - sic to me.

What do they got, a lot ___ of sand.   We got a

Your Cheatin' Heart

Words and Music by Hank Williams

Bridge

you. _____ When tears come down _____ like fall - in'

rain, _____ you'll toss a - round _____ and call my

Chorus

name. _____ You'll walk _ the _ floor _____ the way I

do. _____ Your cheat - in' _ heart _____ will tell on

1.

you. _____ 2. Your cheat - in' _____

2.

Blackbird

Words and Music by John Lennon and Paul McCartney

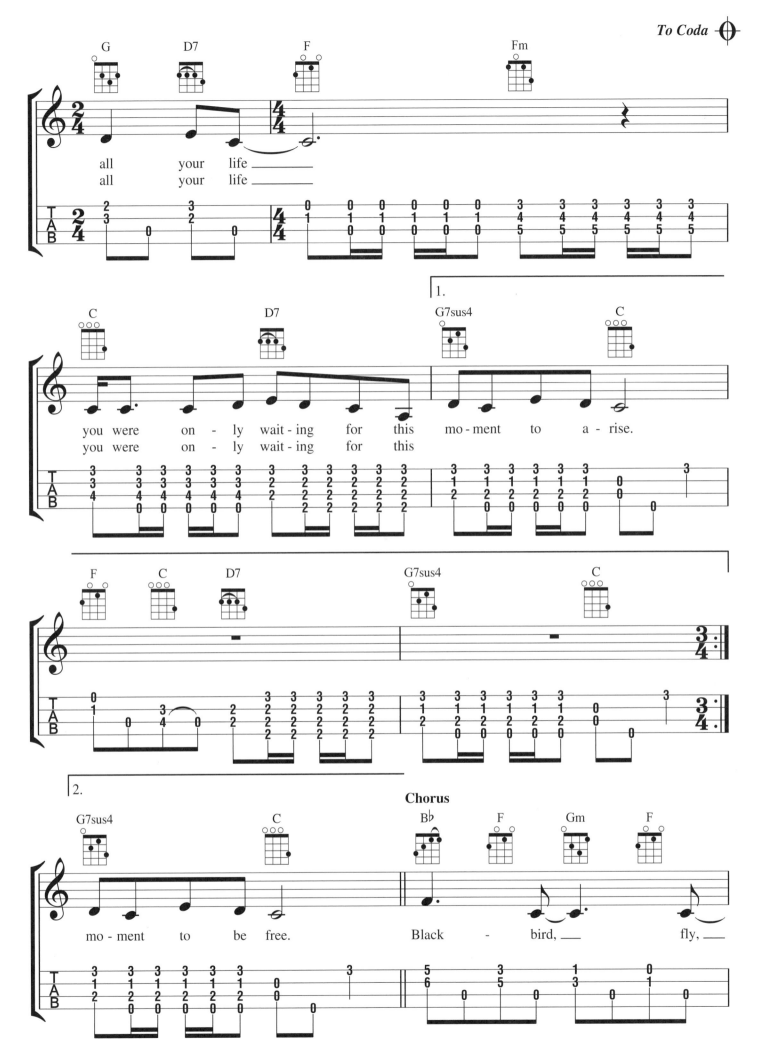

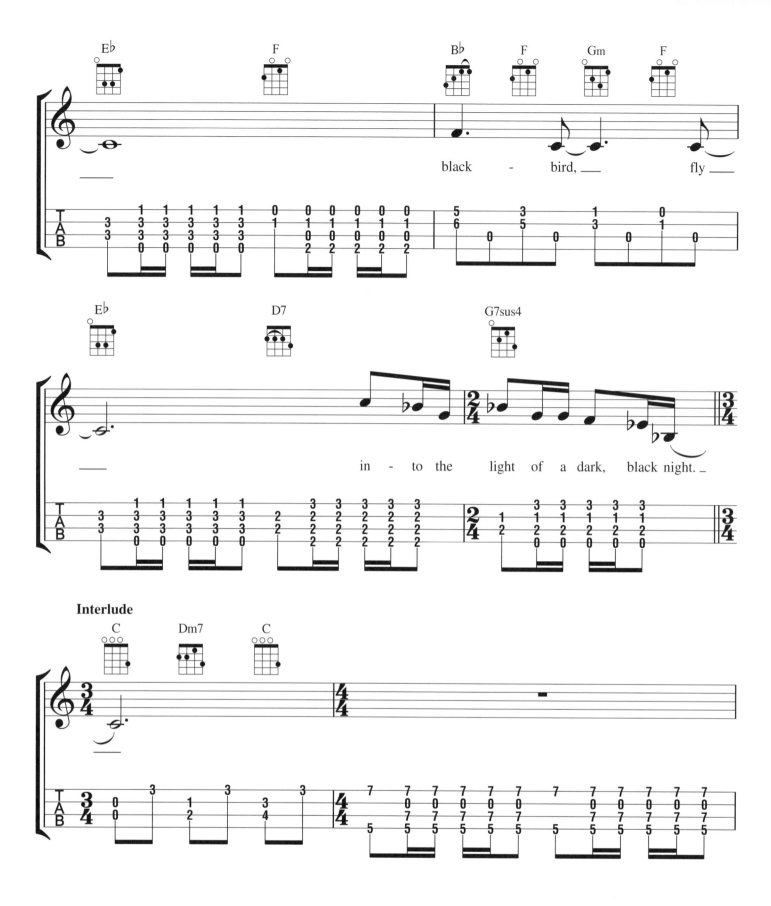

black - bird, ___ fly ___

in - to the light of a dark, black night. _

Interlude

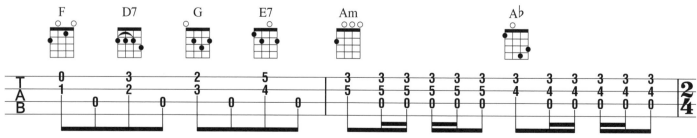

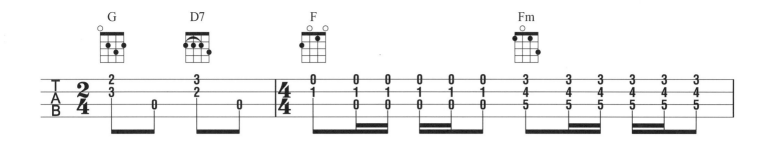

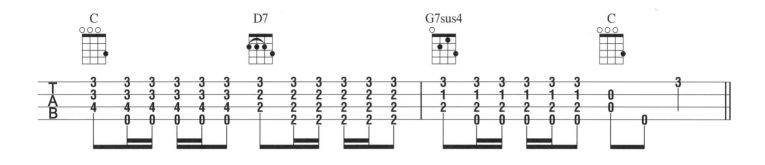

Chorus

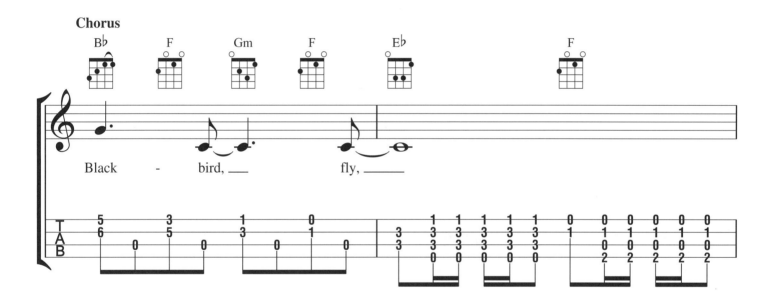

Black - bird, ____ fly, _____

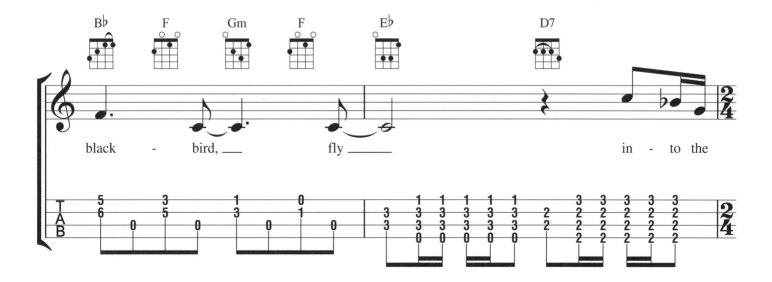

black - bird, ____ fly _____ in - to the

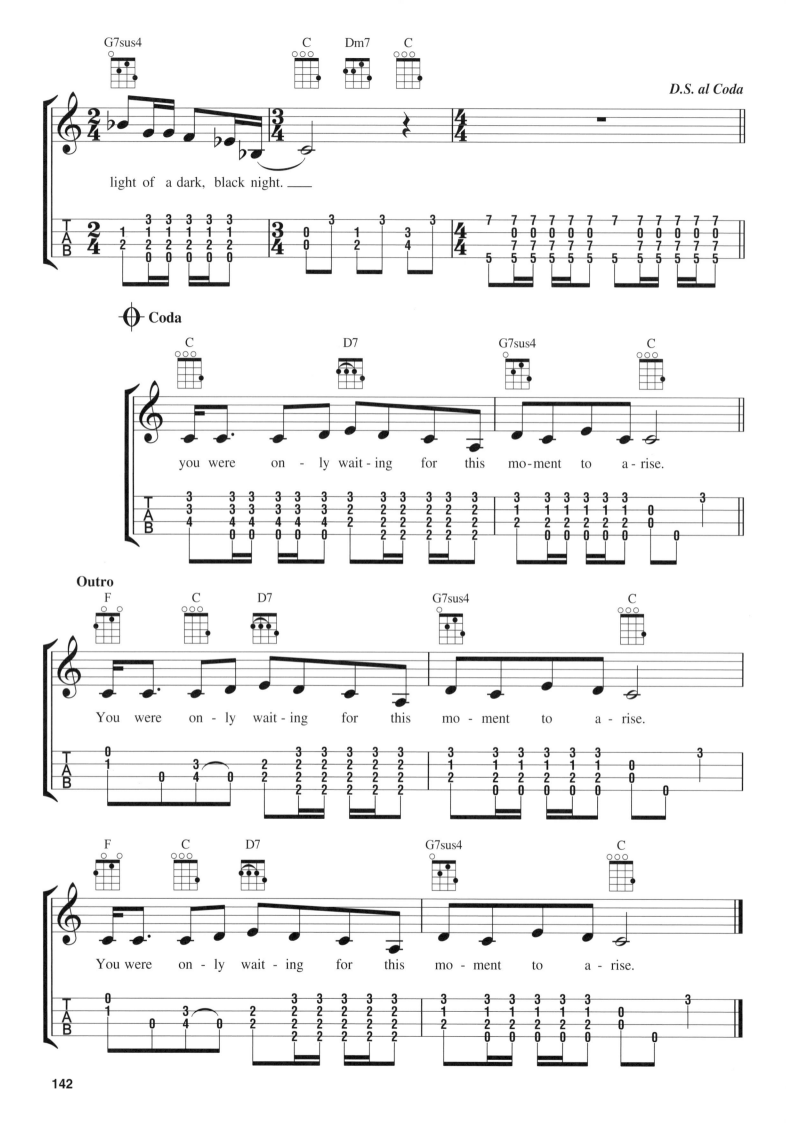

Hey Joe

Words and Music by Billy Roberts

1. Hey _____ Joe,
2., 3. *See additional lyrics*

where you go - in' with that

gun in your hand?

Hey _____ Joe,

I said where you go - in' with that gun in your hand?

I'm go - in' down to shoot my old la - dy, ___

you know I caught her mess - in' 'round with an - oth - er man.

I'm go - in' down to shoot my old la - dy,

you know I caught her mess - in' 'round with an -

3rd time, To Coda ⊕

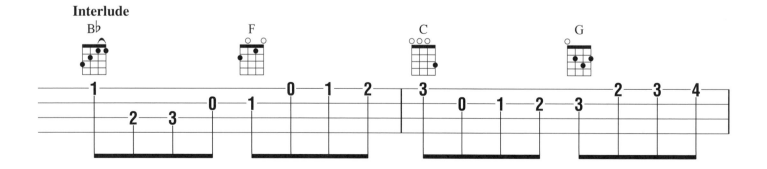

oth - er man.

Interlude

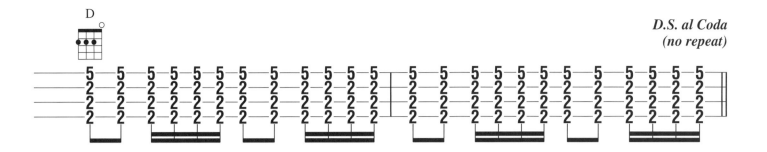

D.S. al Coda
(no repeat)

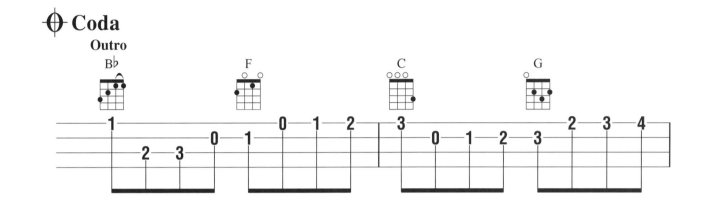

⊕ Coda

Outro

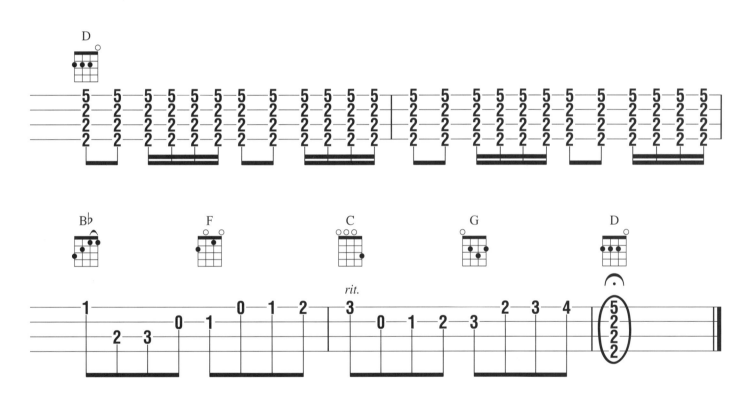

Additional Lyrics

2. Hey Joe, I heard you shot your woman down.
Hey Joe, I heard you shot your old lady down, shot her down in the ground.
Yes I did, I shot her; you know I caught her messin' 'round, messin' 'round town.
Yes I did, I shot her; you know I caught my old lady messin' 'round town.

3. Hey Joe, where you gonna run to now?
Hey Joe, I said, where you gonna run to now?
I'm goin' way down south, way down to Mexico way.
I'm goin' way down south, way down where I can be free.

Daughter

**Words and Music by Stone Gossard, Jeffrey Ament,
Eddie Vedder, Michael McCready and David Abbruzzese**

First note

Intro
Moderately ♩ = 100

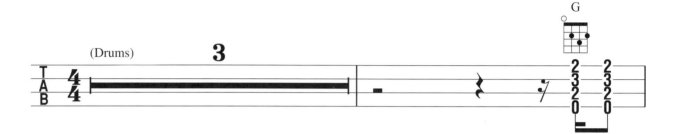

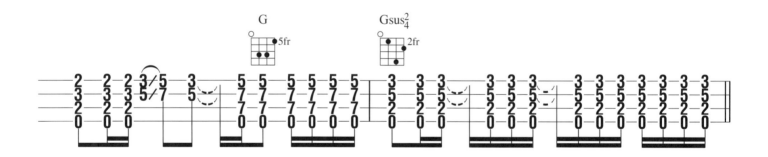

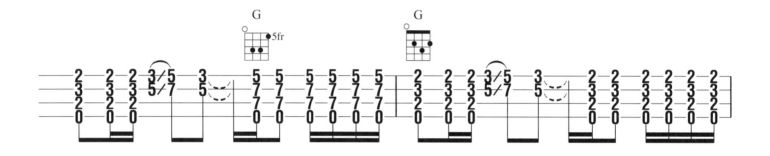

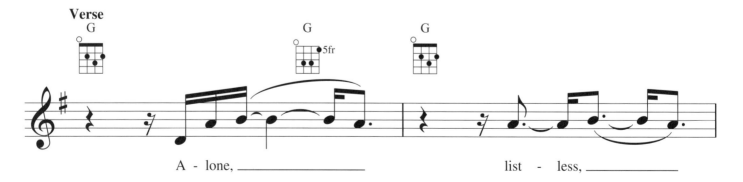

A - lone, _____ list - less, _____

break - fast ta - ble in an oth - er - wise emp - ty room. ___

___ Young ___ girl, ___ vi - o - lins, ___

cen - ter of her own at - ten - tion. ___

Moth - er reads a - loud, ___ child tries ___ to un - der - stand ___ it, ___

___ tries to make ___ her ___ proud. ___

Pre-Chorus

The shades ___ go ___ down. It's in ___ her ___ head, ___

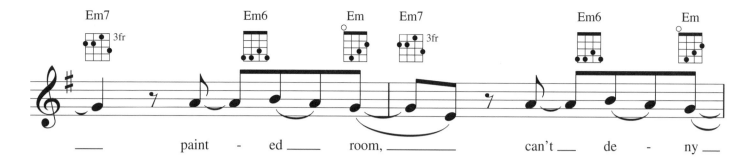

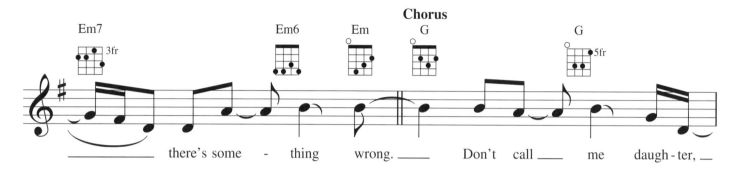

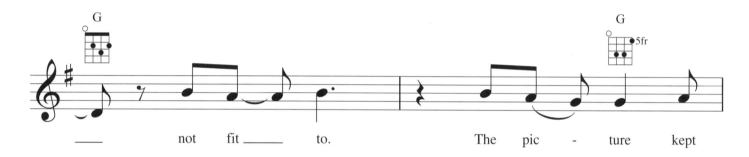

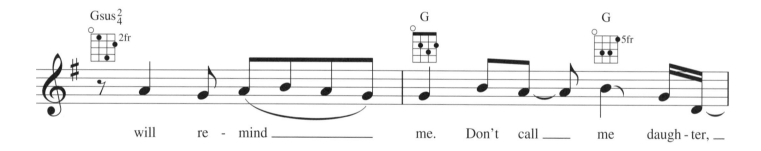

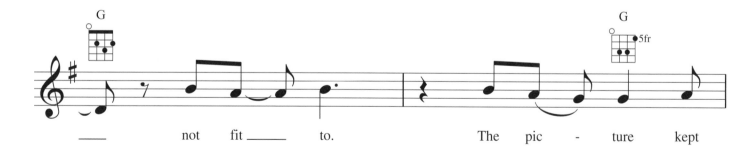

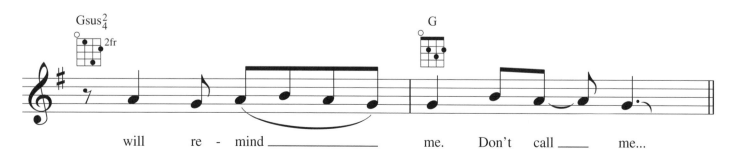

Interlude

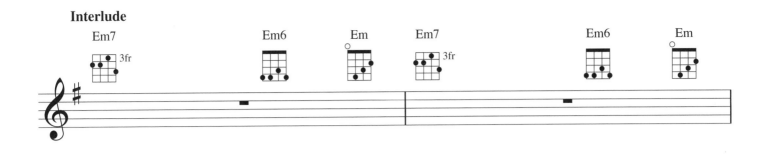

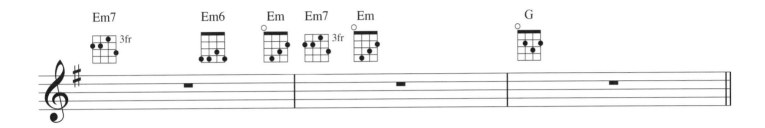

Bridge

She holds ___ the hand ___ that holds ___ her down. ___

___ She will ___ rise ___ a - bove. ___

Guitar Solo

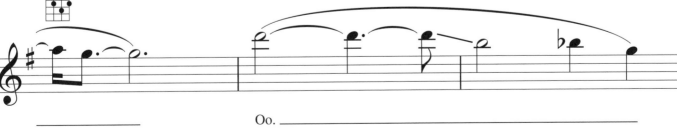

___ Oo. ___

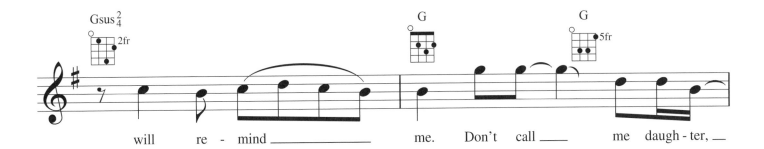

will re - mind _____ me. Don't call ____ me daugh - ter, __

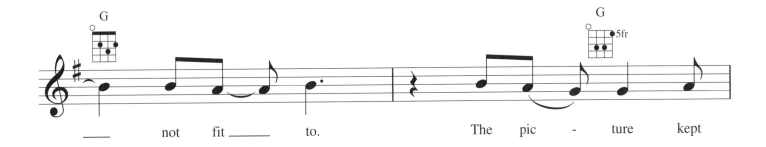

____ not fit ____ to. The pic - ture kept

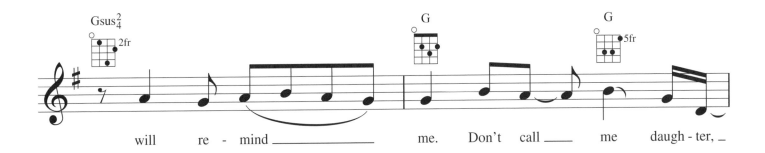

will re - mind _____ me. Don't call ____ me daugh - ter, __

____ not fit ____ to be. ____ The pic - ture kept

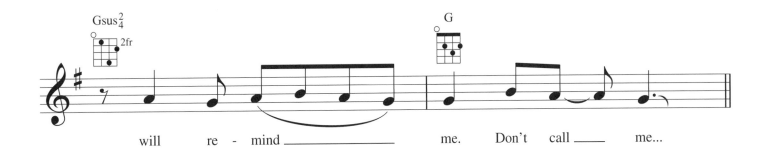

will re - mind _____ me. Don't call ____ me...

Interlude

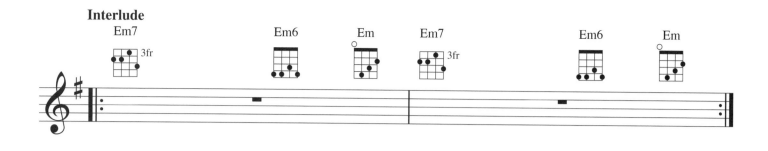

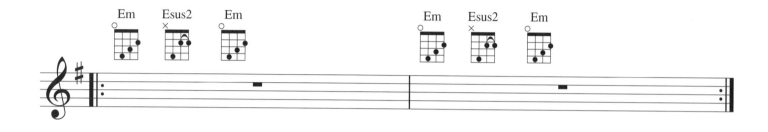

Outro

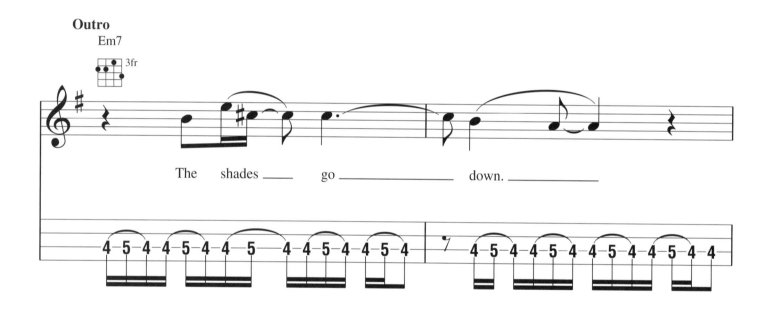

The shades _____ go _____ down. _____

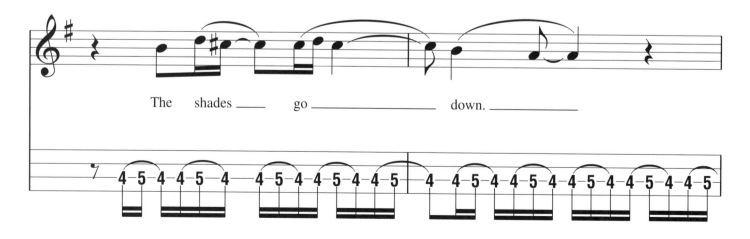

The shades _____ go _____ down. _____

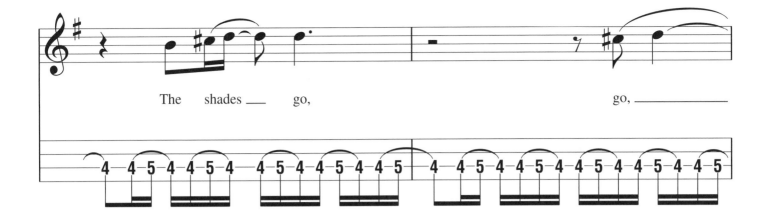

The shades ___ go,   go, _____

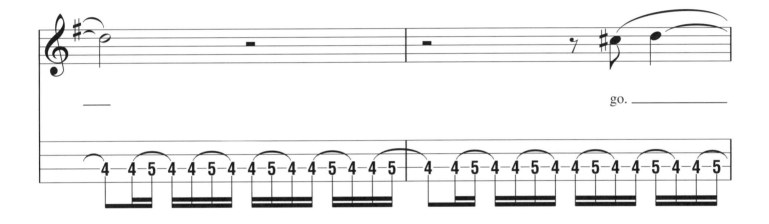

go. _____

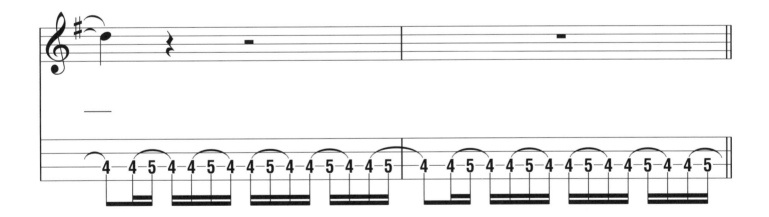

Play 4 times and fade

Heartbreak Hotel

Words and Music by Mae Boren Axton, Tommy Durden and Elvis Presley

though it's al - ways crowd - ed, you still can find ___ some room for

3., 4. *See additional lyrics*

bro - ken - heart - ed lov - ers ___ to cry there in the gloom. ___ We'll be so,

we'll be so lone - ly, ba - by, we'll be so lone - ly.

1., 2.

3.

Well, they're so lone - ly, ___ they could die. 3. Now, the die.

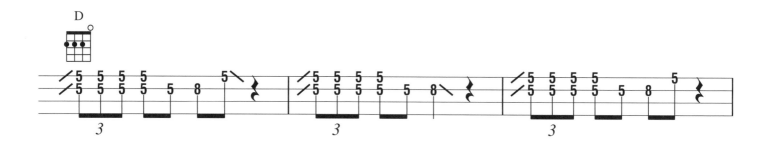

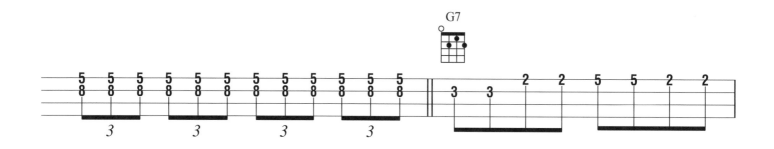

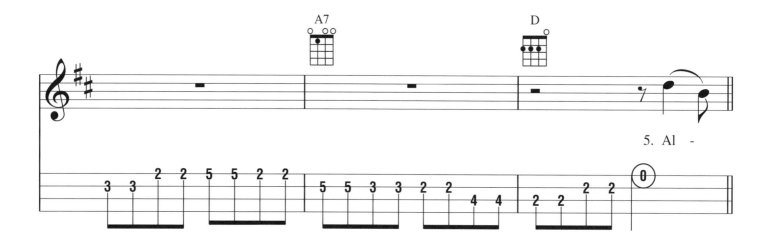

5. Al -

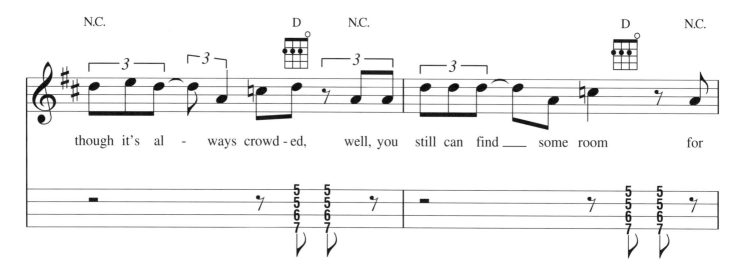

though it's al - ways crowd-ed, well, you still can find ____ some room ____ for

bro - ken - heart - ed lov - ers ___ to cry there in the gloom. ___ We'll be so,

G7

we'll be so lone - ly, ba - by, well, they're so lone - ly, ___

A7   D   N.C.   E♭maj7   Dmaj7
                                                              3fr   2fr

we'll be so lone - ly ___ they could die. ___

Additional Lyrics

3. Now, the bellhop's tears keep flowin', the desk clerk's dressed in black,
   Well, they've been so long on Lonely Street they'll never, never gonna look back and they're so...
   They'll be so lonely, baby. Well, they're so lonely.
   Well, they're so lonely they could die.

4. Well, now if your baby leaves ya and you got a tale to tell,
   Well, just take a walk down Lonely Street to Heartbreak Hotel where you will be...
   You'll be so lonely, baby; where you will be lonely.
   You'll be so lonely you could die.

Rock'n Me

Words and Music by Steve Miller

know in my heart __ I've got to please my sweet ba - by, yeah. __
things that I do __ are gon - na come back to you in your sweet time. __

A

__ 2. Well, I ain't ___ su - per - sti - tious and I
Phoe - nix, Ar - i - zo - na, all the
__ 5. I went from Phoe - nix, Ar - i - zo - na, all the

G

don't get sus - pi - cious, 'cause my wom - an is a friend of mine. ___
way to Ta - co - ma, Phil - a - del - phi - a, At - lan - ta, L. - A., __
way to Ta - co - ma, Phil - a - del - phi - a, At - lan - ta, L. - A., __

D

__ And I know ___ that it's true ___ that all the
__ north - ern Cal - i - for - nia where the
__ north - ern Cal - i - for - nia where the

A

things that I do ___ will come back ___ to me in my sweet
girls are warm __ so I could be with my sweet ba - by,
girls are warm __ so I could hear my sweet ba - by

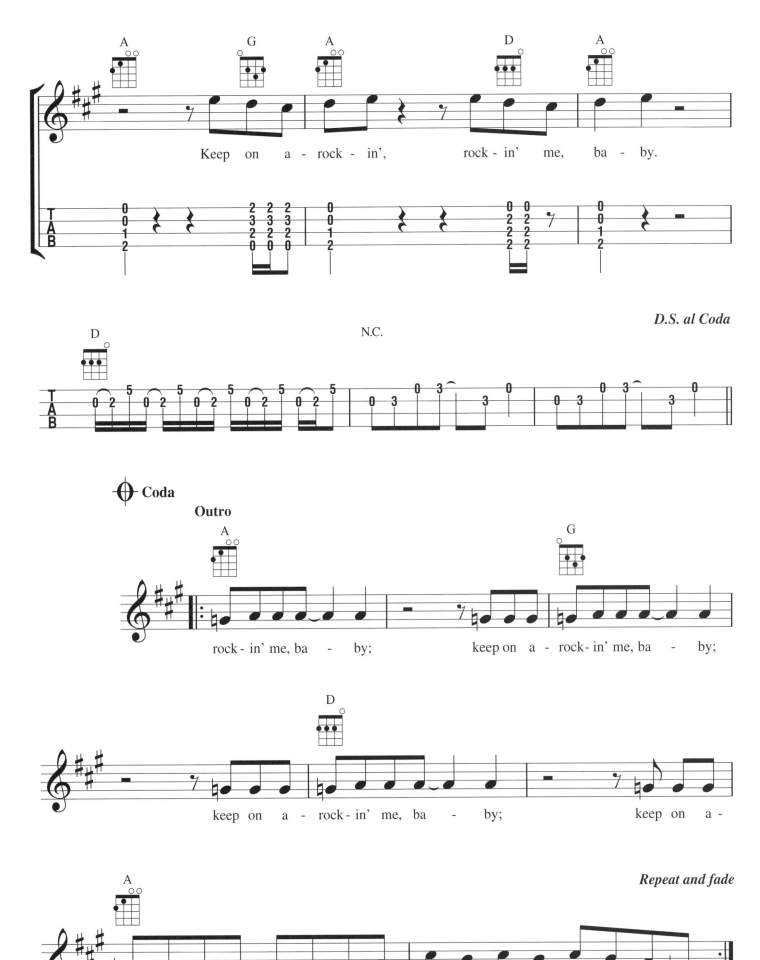

Time in a Bottle

Words and Music by Jim Croce

First note

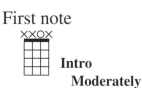

Intro
Moderately

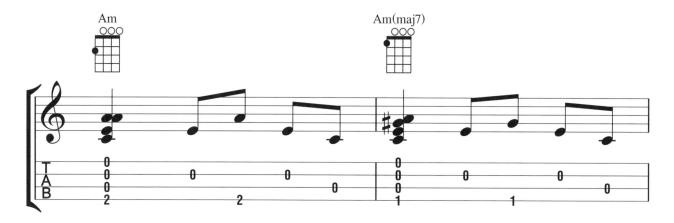

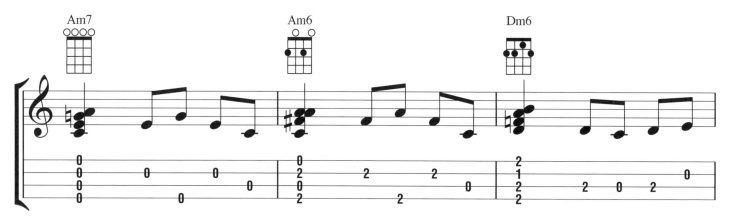

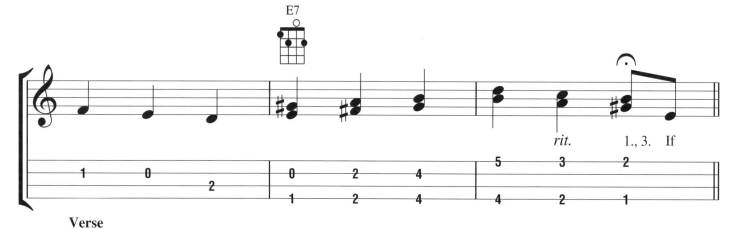

rit. 1., 3. If

Verse

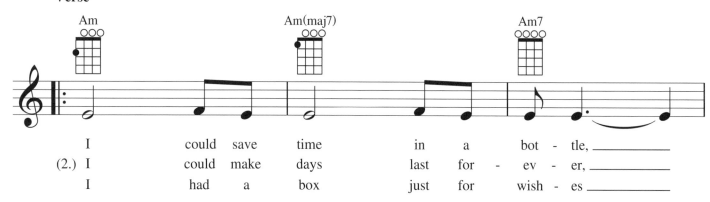

I   could save   time   in   a   bot - tle, _____
(2.) I   could make   days   last   for   ev - er, _____
I   had   a   box   just   for   wish - es _____

the   first   thing _____ that   I'd   like   to   do

if   words   could _____ make   wish - es   come   do

and   dreams ___ that   had   nev - er   come   true.

is   to   save   ev - 'ry   day   'til   e - ter - ni - ty _____

I'd   save   ev - 'ry   day   like   a   treas - ure   and

The   box   would   be   emp - ty   ex - cept   for   the

pass - es   a - way   just   to   spend   them   with

then   a - gain   I   would   spend   them   with

mem - 'ry   of   how   they   were   an - swered   by

1.

2.

you.   2. If   But   there

you.

you.

Bridge

nev - er   seems ___ to   be   e - nough   time ___ to   do   the   things ___ you

want to do once you find them. _____

I've looked a-round e-nough _____ to know _____ that

you're the one I want to go through time with.

To Coda ⊕

D.C. al Coda
(take 2nd ending)

⊕ **C o d a**

Outro

Play 3 times

Wake Me Up When September Ends

Words by Billie Joe
Music by Green Day

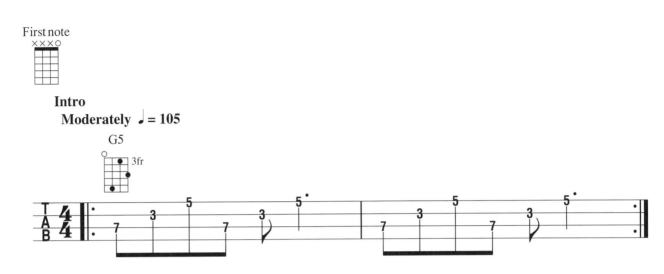

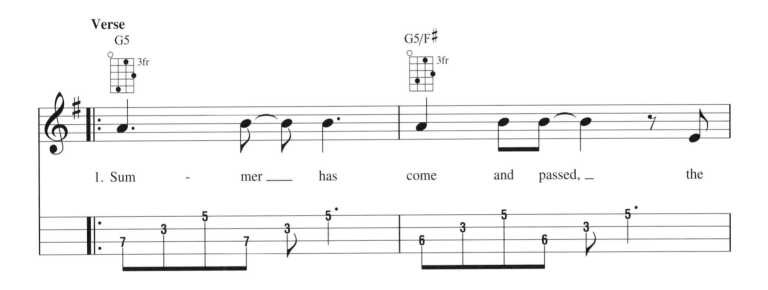

when Sep - tem - ber ends. ___

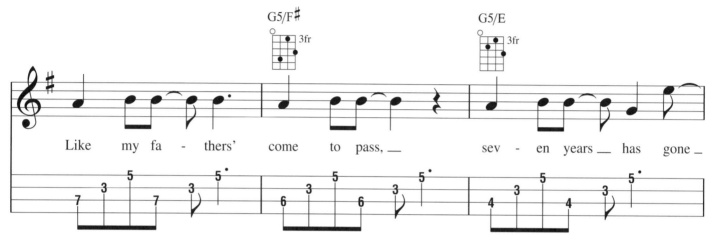

Like my fa - thers' come to pass, ___ sev - en years ___ has gone ___

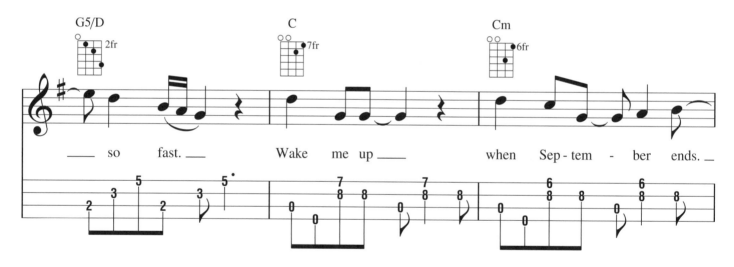

___ so fast. ___ Wake me up ___ when Sep - tem - ber ends. ___

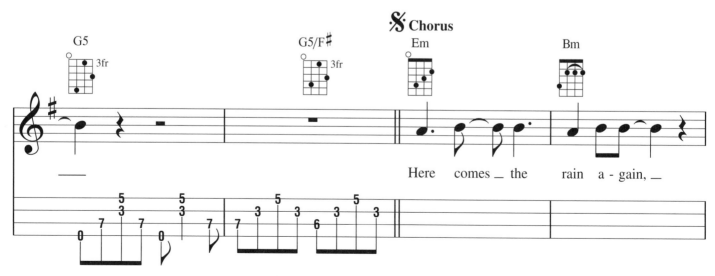

𝄋 Chorus

Here comes ___ the rain a - gain, ___

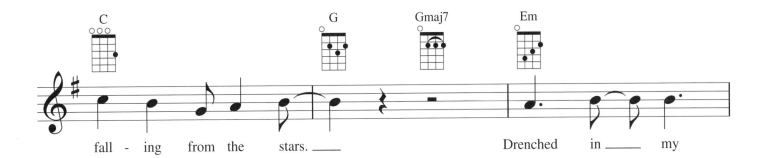

falling from the stars. ____ Drenched in ____ my

pain a - gain, ____ be - com - ing who we ____ are. ____

Verse

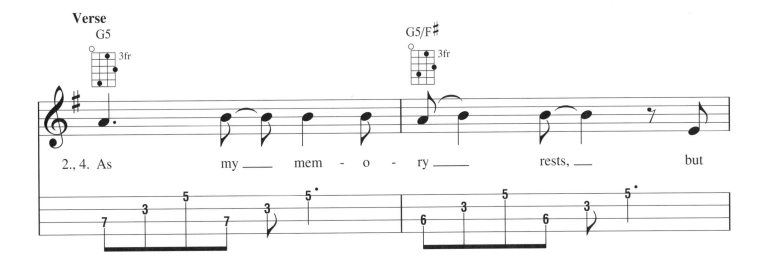

2., 4. As my ____ mem - o - ry ____ rests, ____ but

To Coda ⊕

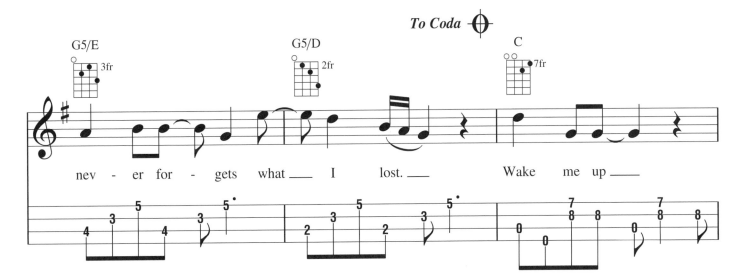

nev - er for - gets what ____ I lost. ____ Wake me up ____

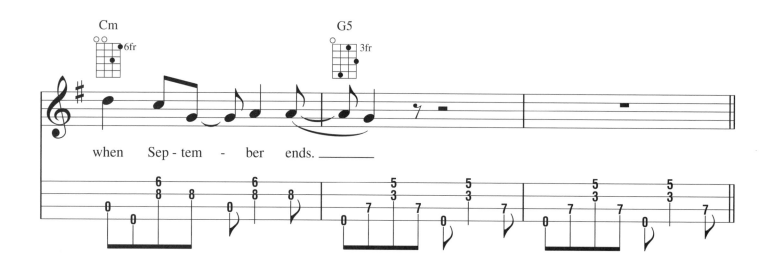

when Sep - tem - ber ends. _____

Interlude

G5

Play 3 times

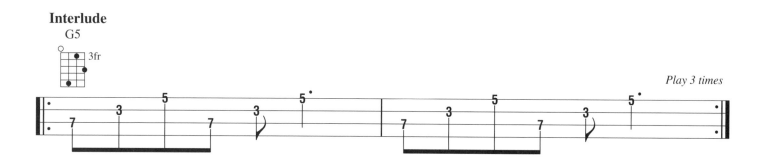

Verse

G5   G5/F♯

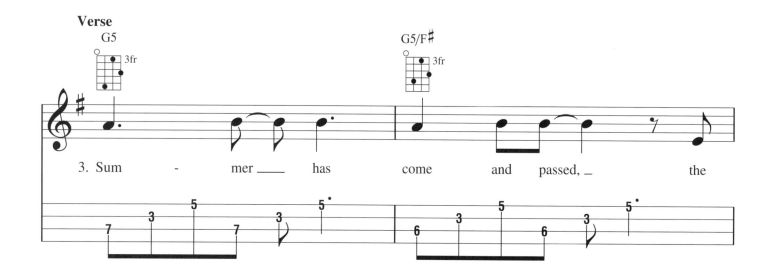

3. Sum - mer ____ has come and passed, __ the

G5/E   G5/D

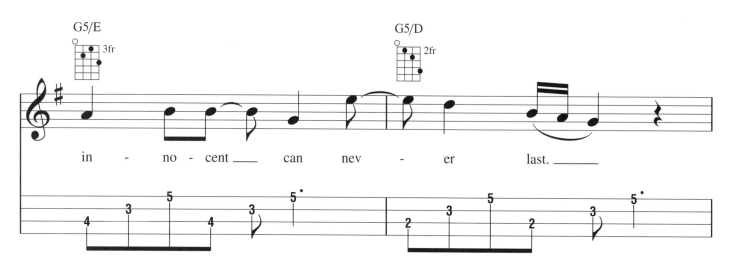

in - no - cent ____ can nev - er last. _____

Wake me up ___ when Sep - tem - ber ends. ___

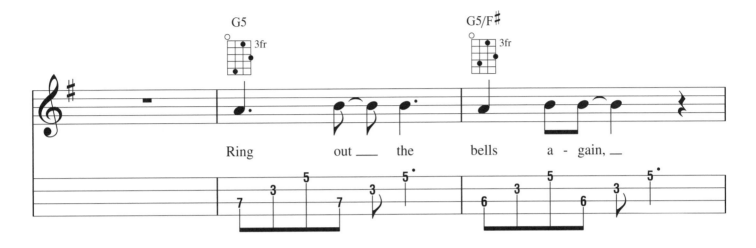

Ring out ___ the bells a - gain, ___

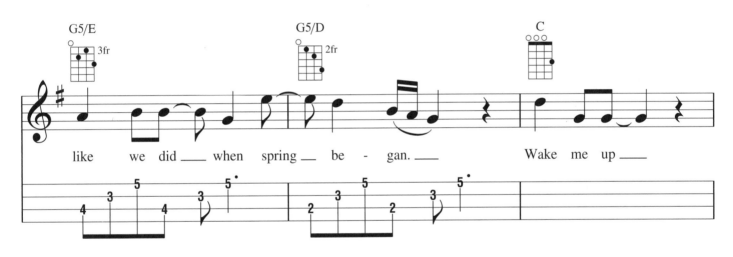

like we did ___ when spring ___ be - gan. ___ Wake me up ___

D.S. al Coda

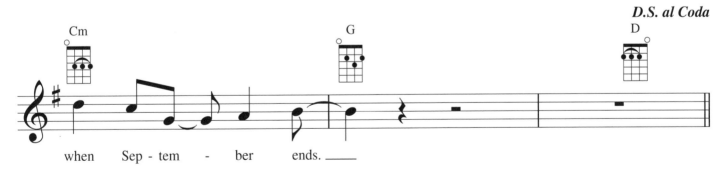

when Sep - tem - ber ends. _____

𝄋 **Coda**

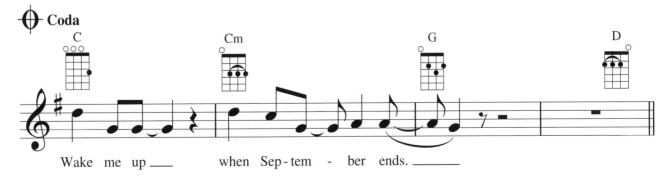

Wake me up ___ when Sep - tem - ber ends. _____

Guitar Solo

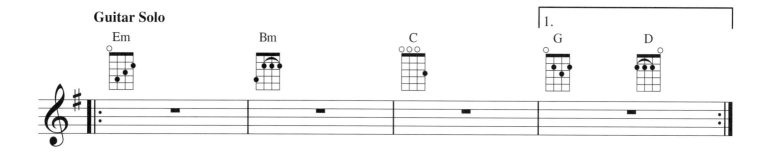

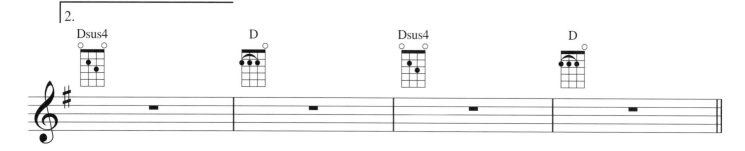

Interlude

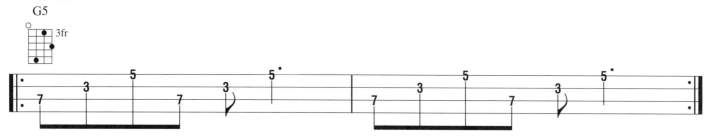

Verse

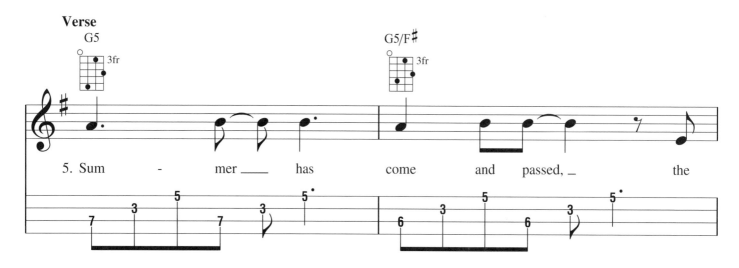

5. Sum - mer ___ has come and passed, ___ the

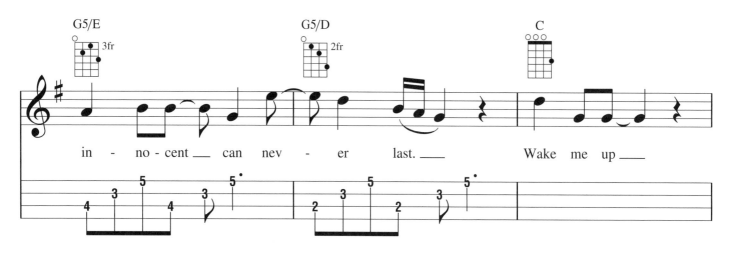

in - no - cent ___ can nev - er last. ___ Wake me up ___

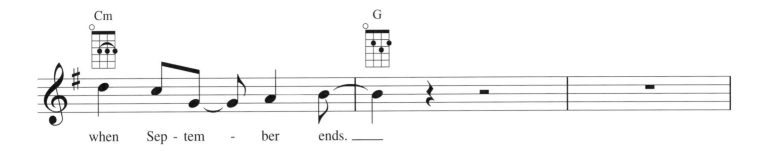

when Sep - tem - ber ends. _____

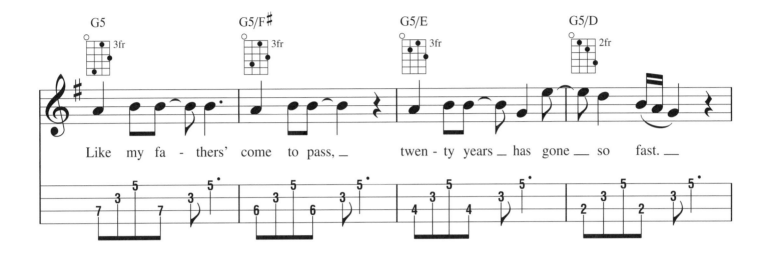

Like my fa - thers' come to pass, _ twen - ty years _ has gone _ so fast. _

Wake me up _____ when Sep - tem - ber ends. _____

Wake me up _____ when Sep - tem - ber ends. _____

Wake me up _____ when Sep - tem - ber ends. _____

Yellow

Words and Music by Guy Berryman, Jon Buckland, Will Champion and Chris Martin

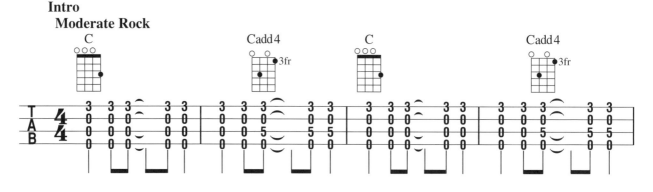

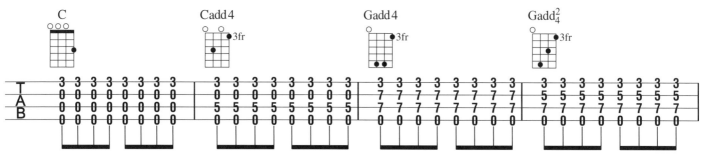

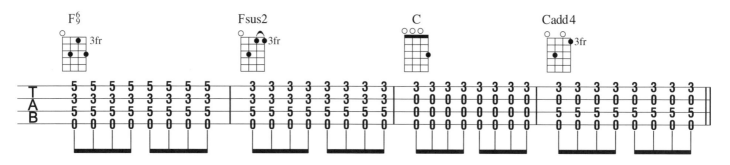

Verse

2. I came a-long; I wrote a song for _____ you
3. I swam a-cross; I jumped a-cross for _____ you.

and all the things you ___ do, ____ and it was called _ "Yel-low." _
Oh, what a thing to ___ do, ____ 'cause you were all ____ yel-low. ____

I drew a line, ____ So then I took my _____ turn.
I drew a line for _____ you.

Oh, what a thing to have done; ___ and it was all ____ yel-low. ___⟩
Oh, what a thing to ___ do; ___ and they was all ____ yel-low. ___⟩

Bridge

Your skin, _____

____ oh yeah, your skin and bones turn-ing _____ to some-thing beau-ti-ful

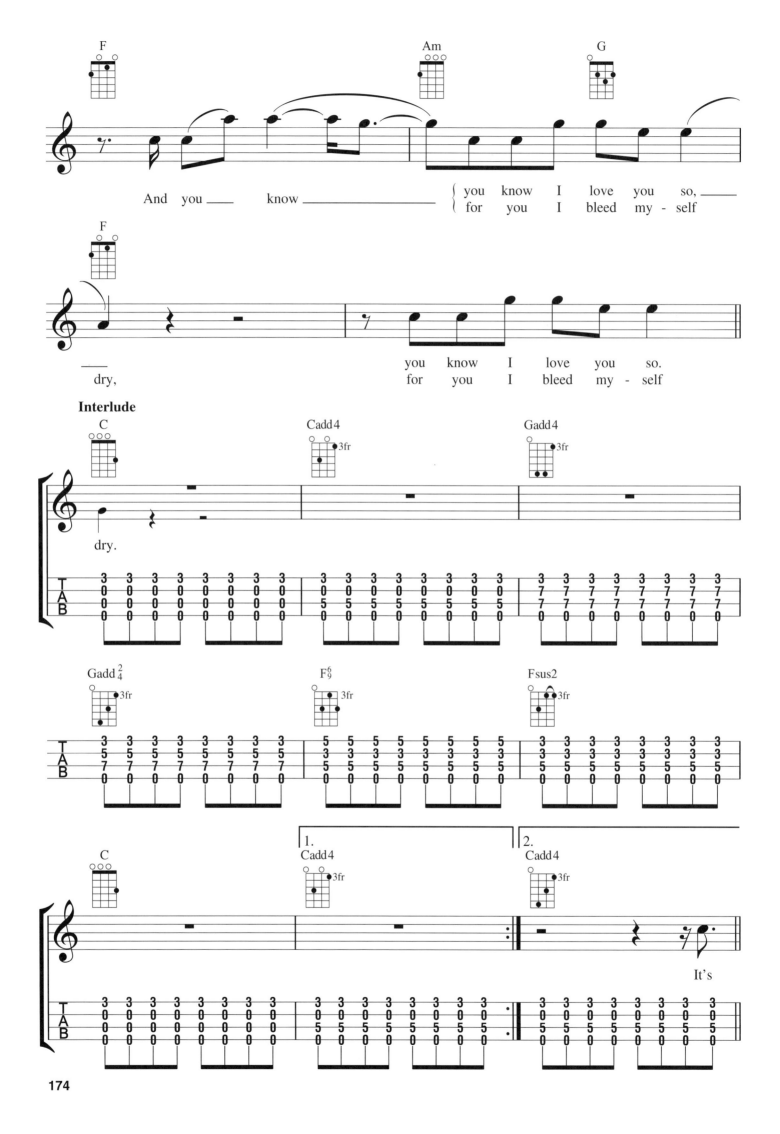

And you ___ know _____ { you know I love you so, ___
                                for you I bleed my - self

___   you know I love you so.
dry,   for you I bleed my - self

Interlude

dry.

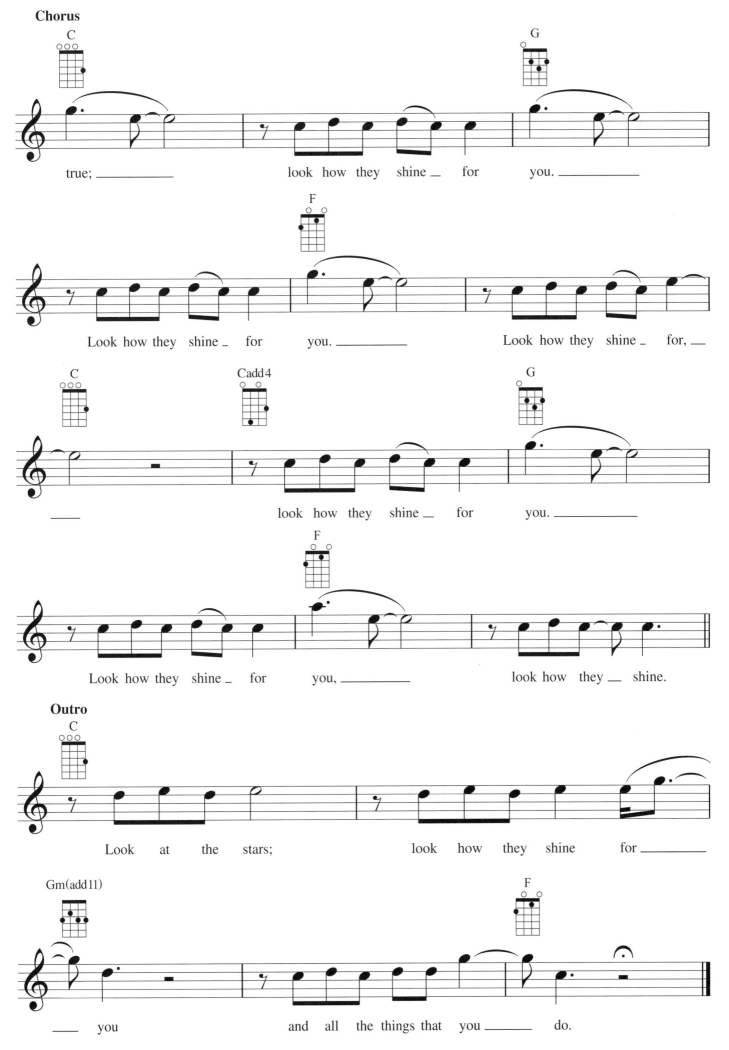

Chorus

true; _____ look how they shine _ for you. _____

Look how they shine _ for you. _____ Look how they shine _ for, __

__ look how they shine _ for you. _____

Look how they shine _ for you, _____ look how they _ shine.

Outro

Look at the stars; look how they shine for _____

___ you and all the things that you _____ do.

Greensleeves

Sixteenth Century Traditional English

Verse
Very slow, in 2

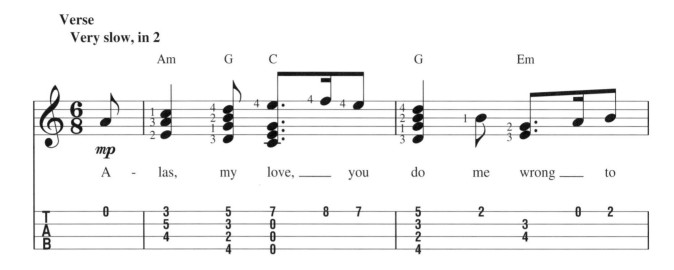

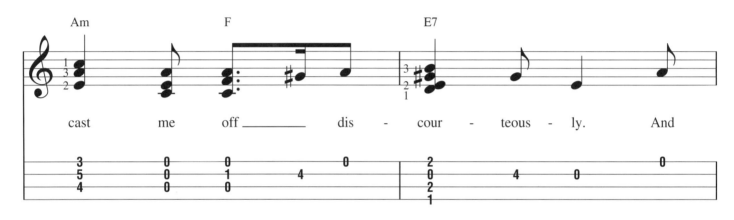

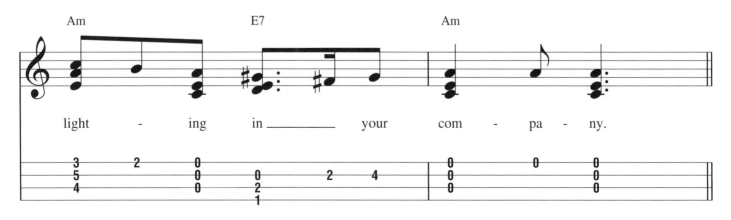

Chorus

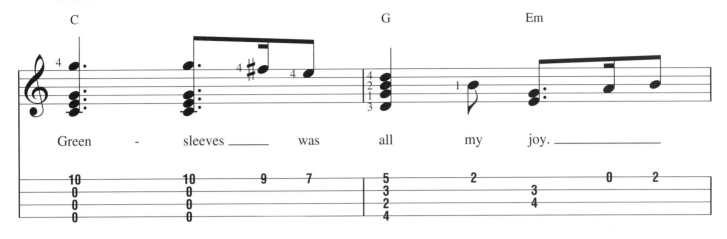

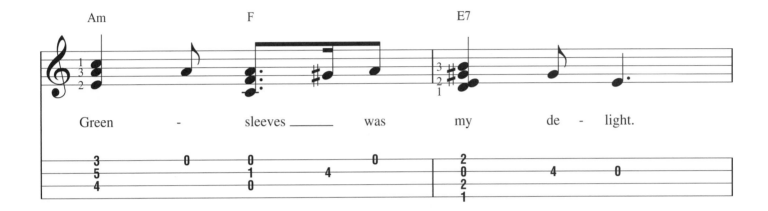

Happy Birthday to You

Words and Music by Mildred J. Hill and Patty S. Hill

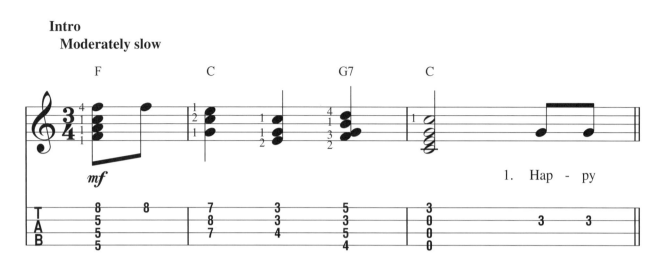

I'll Be There

Words and Music by Berry Gordy, Hal Davis, Willie Hutch and Bob West

Bridge

And oh, _____ I'll be there to com - fort you, build my world ___ of dreams a-round you, I'm so glad that I found you. I'll be there with a love that's strong, I'll be your strength. I'll keep hold - in' on. _____

1st time, D.S. (take repeat)
2nd time, D.S. al Coda

Coda

___ be there.

Outro

Don't you know, ba - by? Yeah, __ yeah, I'll be there. _____

I'll be there. __   Just call my

Repeat and fade

name, __   I'll _____ be there.   Don't you know, ba - by?

Additional Lyrics

3. Let me fill your heart with joy and laughter.
   Togetherness, girl, is all I'm after.
   Whenever you need me, I'll be there.

4. I'll be there to protect you,
   With an unselfish love I'll respect you.
   Just call my name, and I'll be there.

5. If you should ever find someone new
   I know he better be good to you.
   'Cause if he doesn't, I'll be there.

Moondance

Words and Music by Van Morrison

Low G tuning:
(low to high) G-C-E-A

Intro

Moderately fast

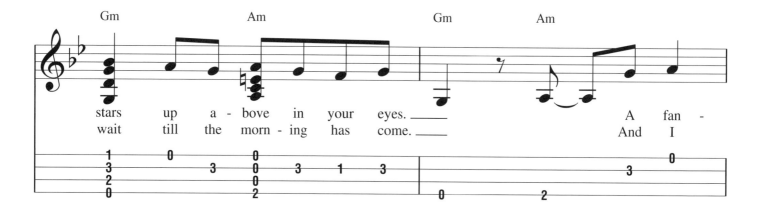

Verse

(3.) mar - vel - ous night ___ for a moon - dance, with the
wan - na make love ___ to you to - night, I can't

stars up a - bove in your eyes. _____ A fan -
wait till the morn - ing has come. _____ And I

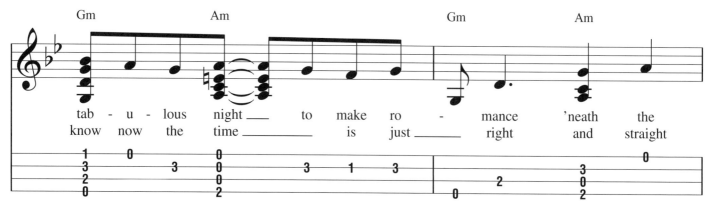

tab - u - lous night ___ to make ro - mance 'neath the
know now the time ___ is just _____ right and the straight

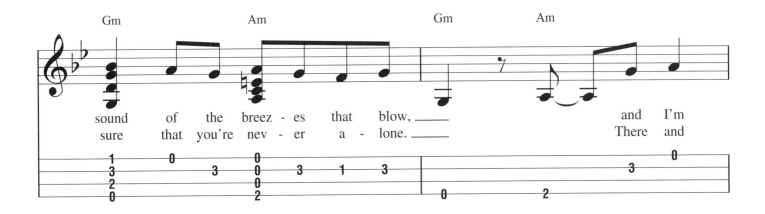

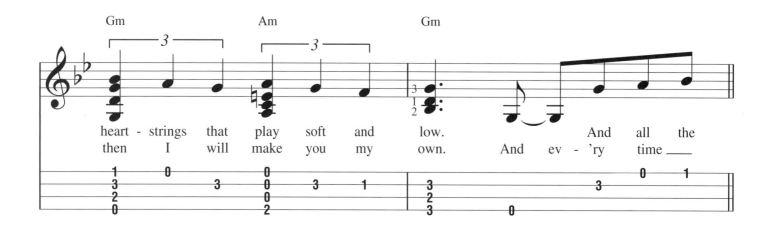

heart - strings that play soft and low. And all the
then I will make you my own. And ev - 'ry time ___

Pre-Chorus

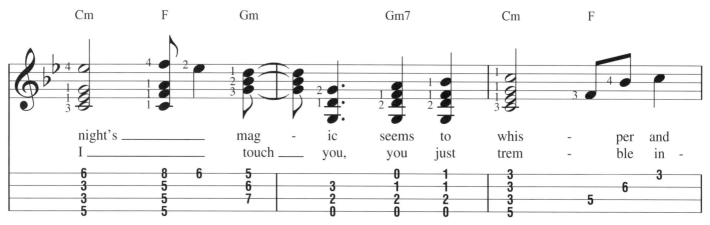

night's _____ mag - ic seems to whis - per and
I _____ touch ___ you, you just trem - ble in -

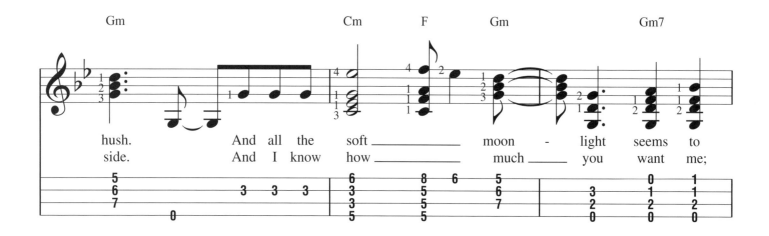

hush. And all the soft _____ moon - light seems to
side. And I know how much _____ you want me;

Chorus

shine in your blush. ___
that you can't hide. ___ Can I just have _ one _

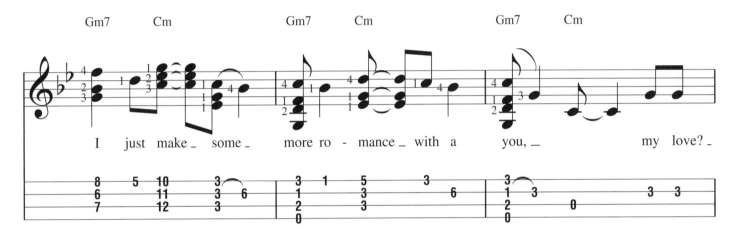

My One and Only Love

Words by Robert Mellin
Music by Guy Wood

Low G tuning:
(low to high) G-C-E-A

Verse
Slow

Bridge

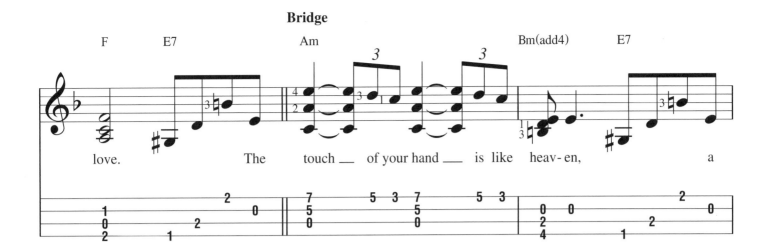

love.   The   touch __ of your hand __ is like   heav-en,   a

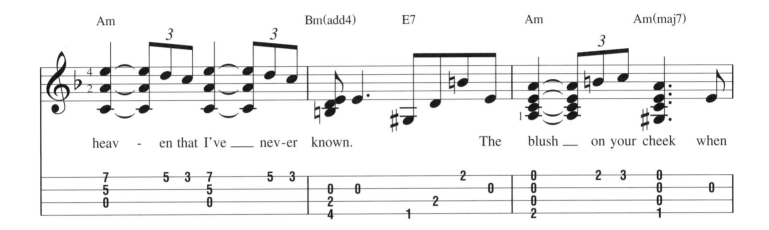

heav - en that I've __ nev-er known.   The   blush __ on your cheek   when

D.C. al Coda

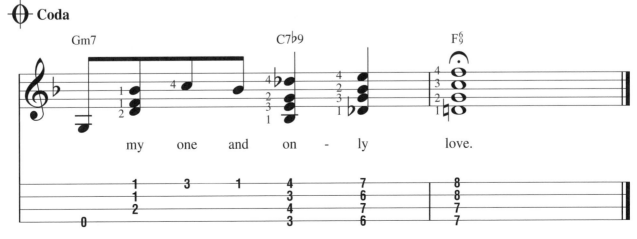

ev - er I speak   tells   me   that   you   are   my   own.

Coda

my   one   and   on - ly   love.

No Woman No Cry

Words and Music by Vincent Ford

Low G tuning:
(low to high) G-C-E-A

Intro

Moderately slow

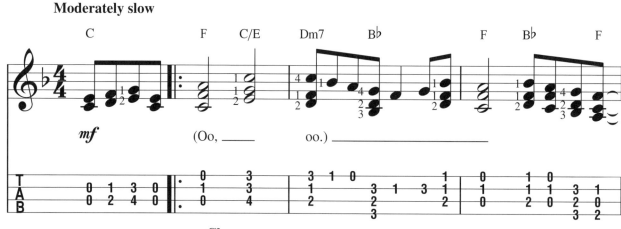

(Oo, _____ oo.)

Chorus

No,
no, wom- an, no cry. _____

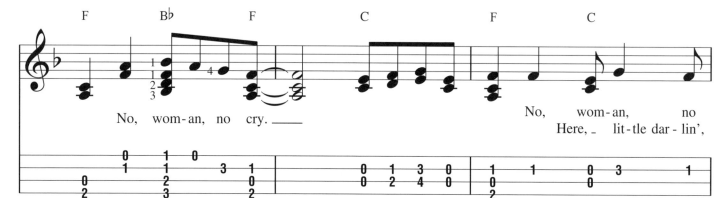

No, wom- an, no cry. _____

No, wom- an, no
Here, _ lit-tle dar - lin',

cry.
don't shed no tears.

No, wom- an, no cry. _____

Said, said.

Verse

1. Said I re - mem - ber when we used __ to sit
2. *See additional lyrics*

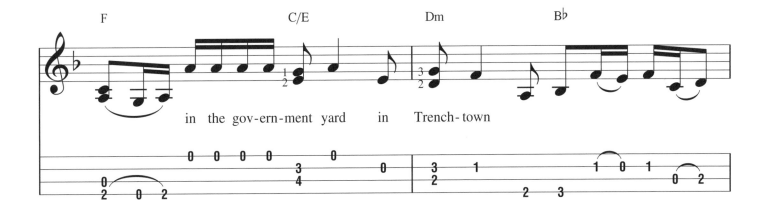

in the gov - ern - ment yard in Trench - town

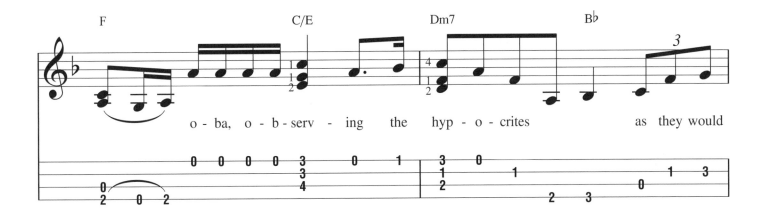

o - ba, o - b - serv - ing the hyp - o - crites as they would

min - gle with the good peo - ple we meet.

Good friends we had, — oh, good friends we've lost

a - long the way. In this bright fu - ture,

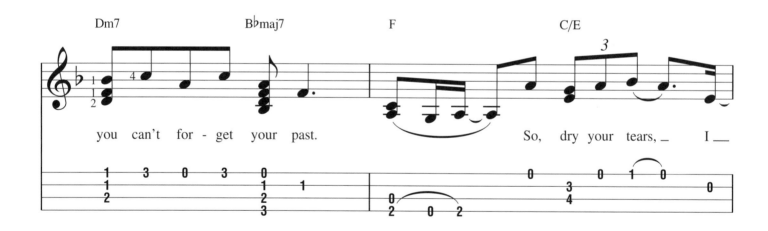

you can't for - get your past. So, dry your tears, — I —

1.

— say. And,

2.

— through, but while I'm gone, I mean...

Bridge

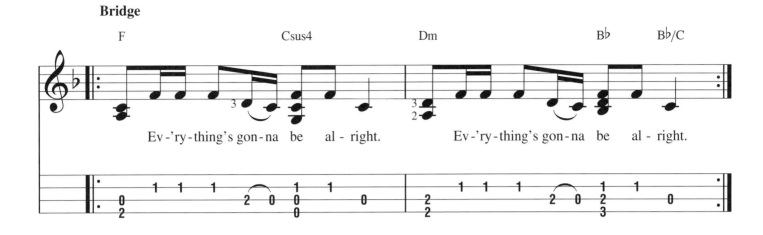

Ev-'ry-thing's gon-na be al - right. Ev-'ry-thing's gon-na be al - right.

Ev-'ry-thing's gon-na be al - right. __ Ev-'ry-thing's gon-na be al - right. __

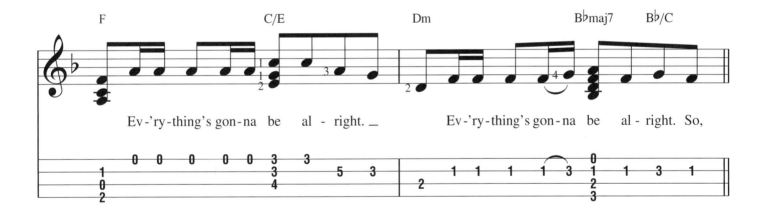

Ev-'ry-thing's gon-na be al - right. __ Ev-'ry-thing's gon-na be al - right. So,

Chorus

wom-an, no cry. No, no, wom-an, no, wom-an, no cry. __

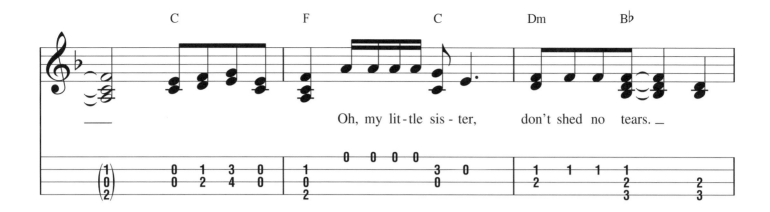

Oh, my lit-tle sis - ter, don't shed no tears. _

Outro

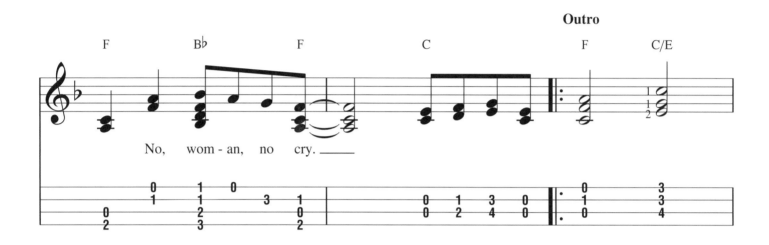

No, wom - an, no cry. _____

Repeat and fade

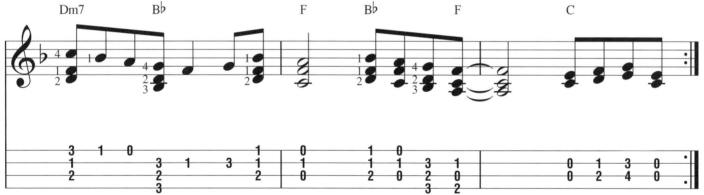

Additional Lyrics

2. Said I remember when we used to sit
In the government yard in Trenchtown,
And then Georgie would make a firelight
As it was logwood burnin' through the night.
Then we would cook corn meal porridge
Of which I'll share with you.
My feet is my only carriage,
So, I've got to push on through,
But while I'm gone, I mean...

Stella by Starlight

from the Paramount Picture THE UNINVITED

Words by Ned Washington
Music by Victor Young

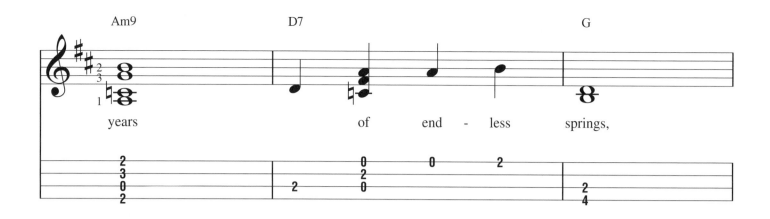

years ... of end - less springs,

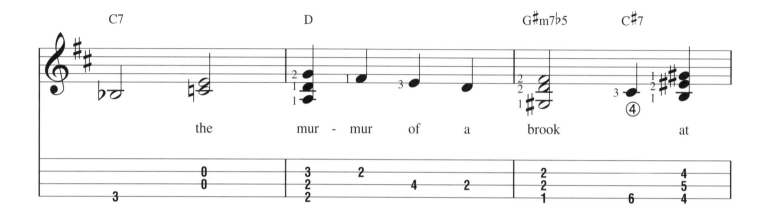

the mur - mur of a brook at

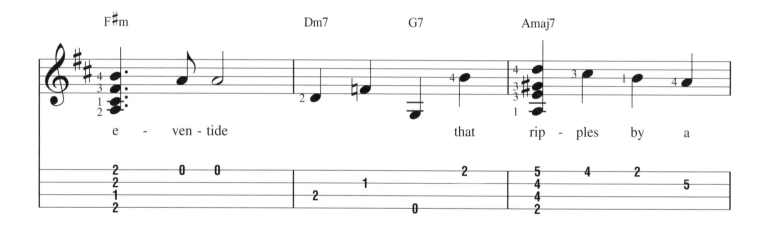

e - ven - tide that rip - ples by a

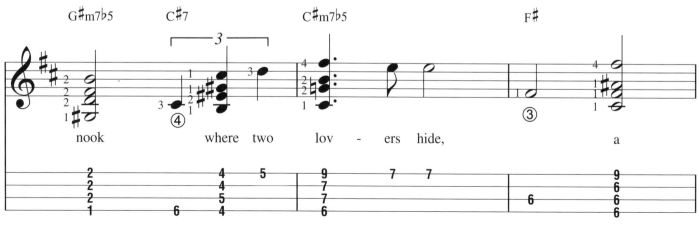

nook where two lov - ers hide, a

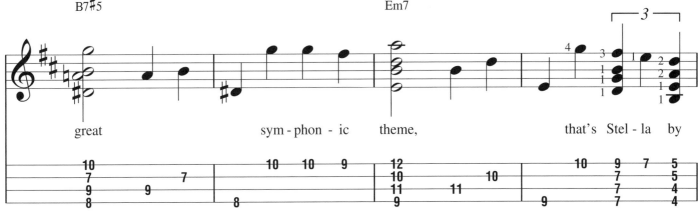

great sym - phon - ic theme, that's Stel - la by

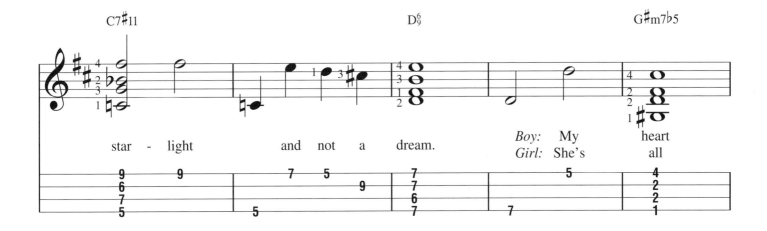

star - light and not a dream.

Boy: My heart
Girl: She's all

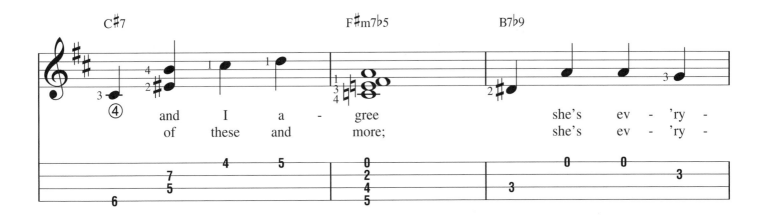

and I a - gree she's ev - 'ry -
of these and more; she's ev - 'ry -

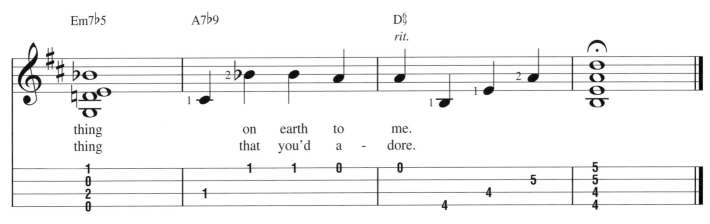

thing on earth to me.
thing that you'd a - dore.

Over the Rainbow

from THE WIZARD OF OZ

Music by Harold Arlen
Lyric by E.Y. "Yip" Harburg

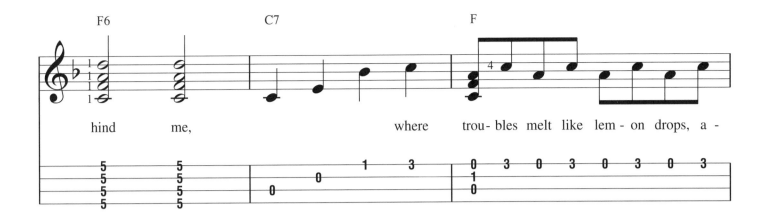

hind me, where trou - bles melt like lem - on drops, a -

D.C. al Coda

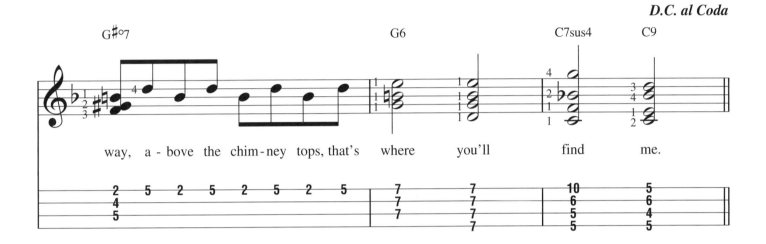

way, a - bove the chim - ney tops, that's where you'll find me.

⊕ **Coda**

Outro
Freely

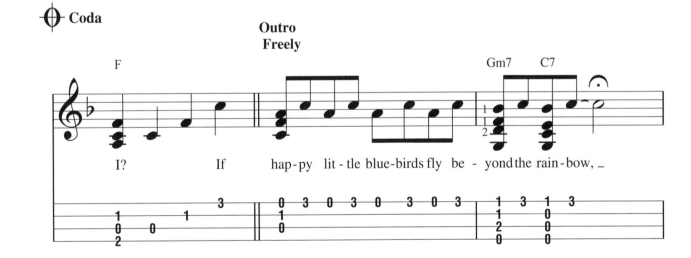

I? If hap - py lit - tle blue - birds fly be - yond the rain - bow, _

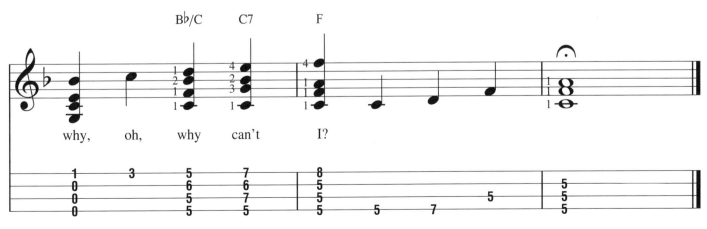

why, oh, why can't I?

People Get Ready

Words and Music by Curtis Mayfield

Low G tuning:
(low to high) G-C-E-A

Intro

Moderately slow

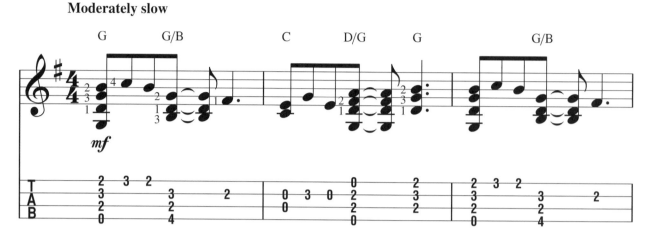

𝄋 Verse

1. Peo-ple get read - y, there's a train a com - in'. You
2., 3., 4. *See additional lyrics*

don't need no bag-gage, you just get on board. __ All you need is faith __ to hear the

Additional Lyrics

2. People get ready for the train to Jordan,
   Picking up passengers from coast to coast.
   Faith is the key, open the doors and board 'em.
   There's room for all among the loved the most.

3. There ain't no room for the hopeless sinner
   Who would hurt all mankind just to save his own.
   Have pity on those whose chances grow thinner
   'Cause there's no hiding place from the Kingdom's throne.

4. So people get ready, for the train's a comin'.
   You don't need no baggage, you just get on board.
   All you need is faith to hear the diesel's hummin'.
   Don't need no ticket, you just, you just thank the Lord.

Brain Damage

Words and Music by Roger Waters

Low G tuning:
(low to high) G-C-E-A

Slow ♩ = 64

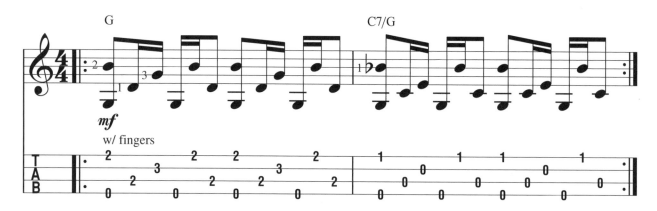

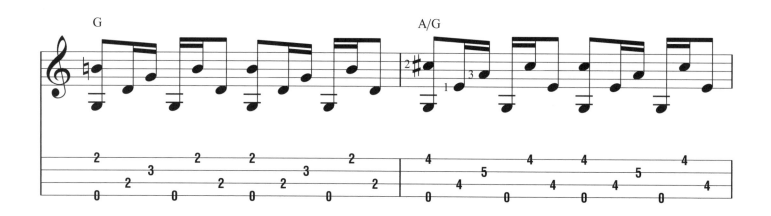

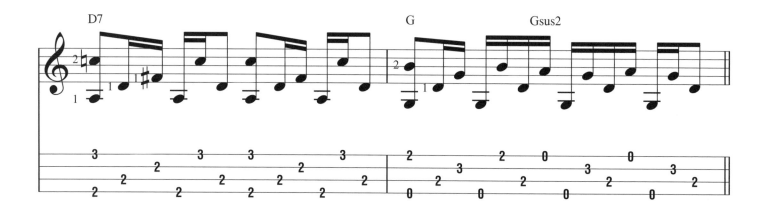

Dust My Broom

Words and Music by Elmore James and Robert Johnson

Low G tuning:
(low to high) G-C-E-A

867-5309/Jenny

Words and Music by Alex Call and James Keller

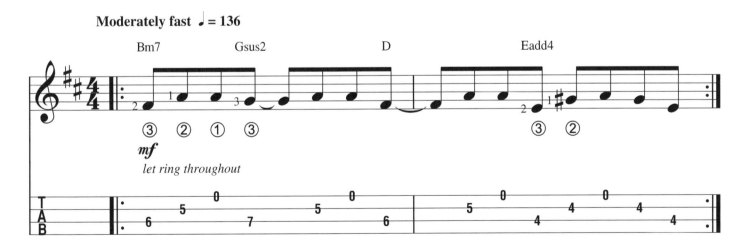

Duelin' Banjos

By Arthur Smith

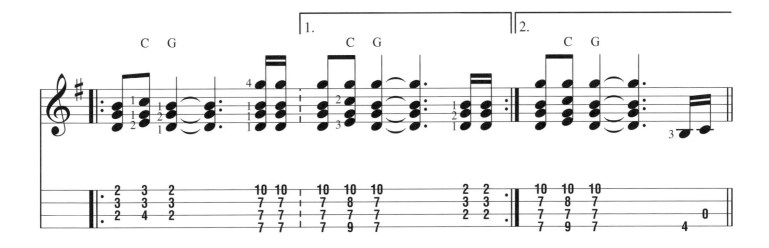

Helter Skelter

Words and Music by John Lennon and Paul McCartney

Low G tuning:
(low to high) G-C-E-A

Moderately slow ♩ = 84

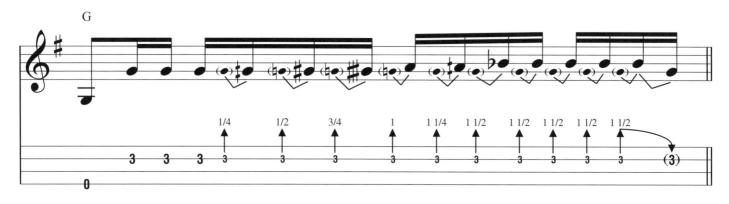

The Man Who Sold the World

Words and Music by David Bowie

Moderately ♩ = 115

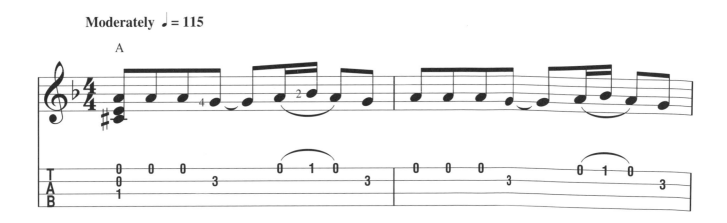

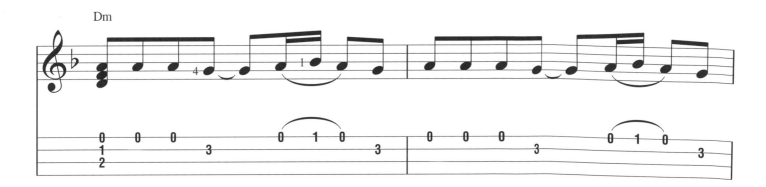

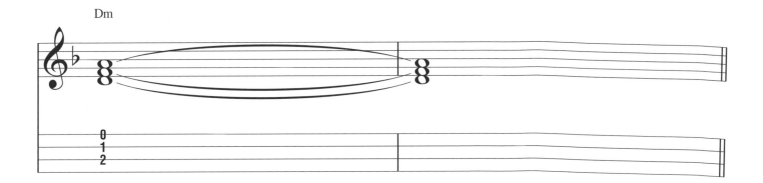

Misirlou

Words by Fred Wise, Milton Leeds, Jose Pina and Sidney Russell
Music by Nicolas Roubanis

Plush

Words and Music by Scott Weiland, Dean DeLeo, Robert DeLeo and Eric Kretz

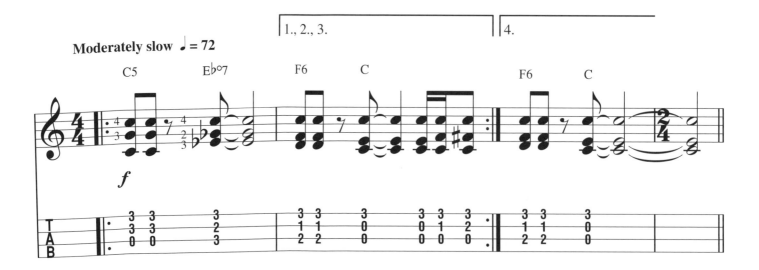

Secret Agent Man

from the Television Series
Words and Music by P.F. Sloan and Steve Barri

Low G tuning:
(low to high) G-C-E-A

Fast ♩ = 160

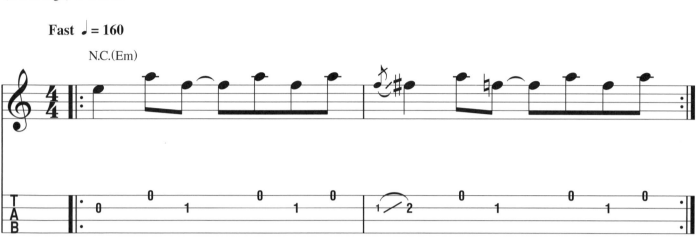

Sunday Bloody Sunday

Words and Music by U2

Moderately ♩ = 100

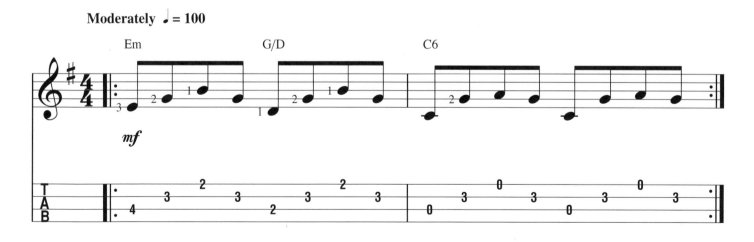

Sunshine of Your Love

Words and Music by Eric Clapton, Jack Bruce and Pete Brown

Low G tuning:
(low to high) G-C-E-A

Moderately ♩ = 112

Ticket to Ride

Words and Music by John Lennon and Paul McCartney

Low G tuning:
(low to high) G-C-E-A

Moderately ♩ = 125

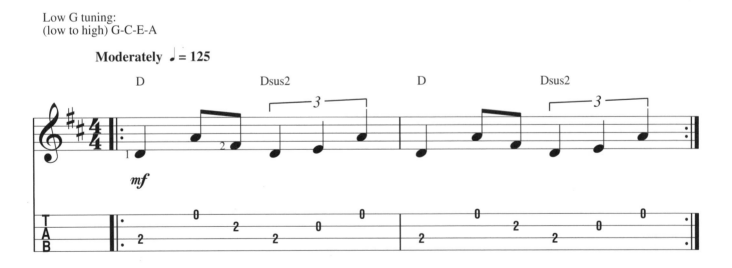